At Identity Automation, effective EdTech coaching [...] safety and security. Our robust identity management an[...] educators to focus on fostering innovation and co[...] in the schools Together, let's build a trusted educational landscape where both coaches and students can thrive.

Identity Automation

#ArchiTech

Aimee Bloom		**Laurie Guyon**
@AJBloom2pnt0		@SMILELearning
@ajbloomedtech.bsky.social		@smilelearning.bsky.social
@ aimee-j-bloom		@guyonsmile
BloomintoEdTech.com		SmileLearningEDU.com

ArchiTech: Laying the Foundation for EdTech Coaching
Copyright © 2025
Written by Aimee Bloom and Laurie Guyon

Edited by Becky Helzer

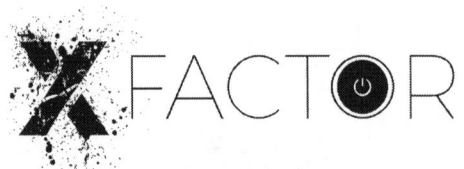

https://xfactoredu.org

Identity Automation

Build the Future of EdTech with Safety and Security at Its Core

The successful use of educational technology in K12 school systems relies on a strong foundation. Safety and security must be our starting point before we can unlock the full potential of innovation and coaching in EdTech. With the right identity management and security systems in place, educators, students, and administrators can collaborate, innovate, and grow with confidence— knowing their data, account access, and digital environments are protected.

Identity Automation

At Identity Automation, we provide the solutions that empower EdTech Coaches to focus on what truly matters: transforming learning experiences. We offer tailored solutions for education, **including:**

 Robust Identity Management

 User-Friendly Single Sign-On (SSO) & Authentication Options

 Compromised Credential Monitoring

 Anti-Phishing Protection

 Network Monitoring

Before creating the ideal digital classroom environment, we must first ensure the systems supporting it are safe, secure, and scalable.

Let's build the future of education together— starting with a foundation of trust.

www.identityautomation.com

Publisher's Note: Dr. Matthew X Joseph

I couldn't be more excited to highlight the amazing work of my friends Aimee Bloom and Laurie Guyon. Over the past six years, I've been lucky enough to get to know them personally and professionally. I'm constantly in awe of their dedication to supporting educators and enhancing learning through technology.

What sets Aimee and Laurie apart is their ability to connect with teachers on a personal level. They don't just show educators how to use tech but how to use it to make learning come alive. Their energy is infectious, their ideas are practical, and they always go above and beyond to make a real difference in classrooms. They're not just about tools; they're about impact.

I've had the privilege of watching them present, and let me tell you, they are dynamic. They bring so much heart and relatability to their work that it's impossible not to be inspired. Laurie's first book, "SMILE Learning," was a joy to publish because it truly reflects who she is—positive, empowering, and dedicated to helping educators thrive. And Aimee brings that same level of passion and insight to everything she does. Together, they're an unstoppable team.

"ArchiTech: Laying the Foundation for EdTech Coaching" is something I'm especially thrilled about. This isn't just another book about technology; it's a guide born out of their real, day-to-day experiences as EdTech coaches. They've poured their hearts into it, sharing strategies, tools, and stories that will resonate with anyone looking to empower educators and improve student learning.

It's been an absolute honor for X-Factor to be the publisher for this project. More than that, though, being their friend means the most to me. Aimee and Laurie are the kind of people who lift others up, and their work will leave a lasting impact on education. I'm so proud of them and can't wait to see how their book inspires educators everywhere.

About the ArchiTechs

Aimee Bloom

Aimee Bloom is the Supervisor of Instructional Technology at Buffalo Public Schools in Buffalo, New York, with over two decades of experience in education. Her career began as a PreK-8th grade art and computer teacher, evolving into roles focused on educational technology, leadership, and professional development. Passionate about improving education, Aimee has participated on committees where she co-authored the NYSED CSDF standards and the Diocese of Buffalo computer technology curriculum. She is also a part of several professional organizations. In her free time, you can often find her on her bike, with her family, or floating on her yak!

Laurie Guyon

Laurie Guyon is the Lead Coordinator for Instructional Tech Programs at WSWHE BOCES in New York, and the Capital Region Director and trainer for NYSCATE. She teaches CS Methods at Manhattanville University and is the author of SMILE Learning: Leveraging the Power of Educational Technology. Laurie co-hosts the SMILE Factor podcast. SAANYS recognized Laurie in 2023 as the Leader in Digital Education and was named a 20 To Watch by ISTE. Laurie contributed to the NYSED authoring committee for the CSDF standards. Outside of work, she enjoys reading and spending time with her family and dog, Paisley.

Becky Helzer: Editor

Becky Helzer is an experienced editor and copy editor who loves working with writers to help them express their ideas clearly and authentically. She has edited a diverse range of content, from curriculum and books to magazine articles and blog posts, beginning her career later in life when her kids were in high school. A proud Colorado native and graduate of Colorado State University's journalism program, Becky lives in Fort Collins with her husband and their two rescue dogs. When she's not engrossed in a good book, she is passionate about baking—especially cinnamon rolls—and exploring her city's extensive bike trail system.

Aimee's Dedications

It's amazing because when asked, "What is your greatest accomplishment?" my answer is always you —my children— Anthony, Ary, and Gavin. You are my everything. Let me leave you with this:

"You know, sometimes all you need is twenty seconds of insane courage. Just literally twenty seconds of just embarrassing bravery. And I promise you, something great will come of it."
- Benjamin Mee, We Bought a Zoo

To Adam, thank you for supporting me and my "homework," crazy ideas, and always challenging me to be the best version of myself.

Laurie's Dedications

I want to express my heartfelt gratitude to my husband and children for their steadfast support and understanding. Your patience and love empower me to pursue my education and technology interests passionately. You bring immense joy into my life, and I could not navigate my professional journey or fully embrace my career without your encouragement. You help me cultivate a balance between my work and personal life, and your presence brings a smile to my face every day. Thank you for being my greatest motivators.

To Matthew X Joseph, thank you for believing in my wild ideas and seeing the potential in me that I never knew existed. Your unwavering encouragement and willingness to open doors I thought would forever remain closed have transformed my educational journey. I am endlessly grateful for your faith in me and for inspiring me to reach for the extraordinary.

Acknowledgments

NYSCATE—Thank you to NYSCATE (The New York State Association for Computers and Technologies in Education). The strength and camaraderie of the NYSCATE Professional Learning Network (PLN), which we affectionately refer to as our Professional Learning Family (PLF), have been invaluable in enhancing our understanding of effective educational technology integration and coaching. Thank you to Mary Beth Guthrie and Amy DelCorvo for allowing us to support educators on their journeys in technology and coaching. We are deeply grateful for their unwavering support and visionary leadership, which continue to inspire and guide our efforts.

Matthew Joseph—We are deeply grateful to Matt Joseph for his unwavering belief in our project, consistent support, and invaluable contributions. We especially appreciate his early morning text messages, exceptional communication skills, and remarkable ability to foster collaboration.

Becky Helzer—To Becky Helzer, our editor: Thank you for your flexibility, dedication to a quick turnaround, and belief in our vision. We are grateful for your expertise and guidance.

Deann Poleon—We are forever grateful to Deann. Her organizational talents made our co-presentations successful, her laughter brightened every moment, and her dedication to students inspired us. We cherish her friendship and the profound impact she has made on the lives of countless students throughout her career.

EdTech Ladies +1—A special-shout out to the EdTech Ladies +1. This group has become an invaluable source of support, laughter, and inspiration. We cherish the camaraderie, shenanigans, and positive impact on our personal and professional growth.

FETC—We deeply appreciate the Future of Education Technology Conference (FETC). This conference holds a special place in our hearts, as it was at a previous FETC that Aimee and Laurie's friendship blossomed. Each FETC experience has been truly enriching, and we are deeply honored to launch our book at this esteemed event. We thank Jennifer Womble, a visionary leader whose dedication to empowering women in technology and education has created countless opportunities, building a legacy of innovation and empowerment. Thank you for creating such a vibrant and impactful community within the EdTech landscape and providing us with this incredible platform to share our work.

We are incredibly grateful to the many individuals and experiences that have shaped our journey. From the students who inspire us every day to the vendors who share their expertise, each interaction has contributed to our growth and helped build our vibrant PLN. We specifically recognize the significant impact of Model Schools through BOCES in New York State. These experiences have greatly enhanced our understanding of education and provided us with the knowledge and skills necessary to succeed as EdTech coaches. We are truly thankful for this collective journey.

ArchiTech
Laying the Foundation for EdTech Coaching

Aimee Bloom & Laurie Guyon
2025

Foreword by Stephanie Howell

Draw, type, or record your work– get instant AI feedback.

Snorkl AI `Correct` `3/4 - Strong`

Great work in multiplying by the conjugate of the denominator! 🫳

Simplify. Answer in complex

$$\frac{4}{5 + 2i} \frac{(5-2i)}{(5-2i)} = \frac{20-8i}{}$$

We distribute the 4 on the numerator

The #1 multimodal AI tool for the classroom

Try as a student:

Table of Contents

Foreword by Stephanie Howell
Ⓧ @mrshowell24

Get ready to embrace your inner Sherpa as you discover new ways to support every teacher - not just the innovative ones eager to try the latest tech tools. So often, we get caught up in the strategies and forget that at the heart of coaching lies the powerful connection between people. Aimee Bloom and Laurie Guyon invite us to slow down and explore effective coaching. Their Book ArchiTech: Laying the Foundation for EdTech Coaching is a resource whether you are a seasoned coach or just starting out.

In this book, authors Aimee Bloom and Laurie Guyon share their real-world experiences and insights, offering a practical blueprint for those entering or seeking to improve their coaching practices. This isn't about the next big edtech gadget; it's all about the people. They explore the pedagogy and how we can best support the educators we coach to personalize the way they learn.

As a coach, you've probably wondered if you're "doing it right." It can feel lonely at times, and you might worry about asking the wrong questions. Fear not! Aimee and Laurie are here to guide you, empowering coaches and the teachers they support to foster creativity and drive meaningful change in schools. They tackle tough topics like roadblocks, time management, and getting teachers excited about professional learning. But they also remind us of the importance of relationships, feedback loops, and leveraging individual strengths. It's a refreshing take that goes beyond the "how-to" and delves into the heart of what it means to be an effective, empathetic coach.

Here are some more tips to help you become a great coach:

- **Listen actively:** Pay attention to what teachers are saying, both verbally and non-verbally. Ask open-ended questions to encourage them to share their thoughts and feelings.
- **Provide constructive feedback:** Offer specific, actionable feedback that helps teachers improve their practice. Be positive and supportive, and focus on strengths as well as areas for growth.
- **Set clear goals:** Work with teachers to set specific, measurable, achievable, relevant, and time-bound (SMART) goals.
- **Celebrate successes:** Acknowledge and celebrate teachers' achievements, no matter how small. This will help to boost their motivation and confidence.
- **Be patient and persistent:** Change takes time. Be patient with teachers as they work to improve their practice. Continue to offer support and encouragement, even when progress seems slow.

So, get ready to redefine your role, embrace learner variability, and use coaching models and cycles to truly make a difference. This book isn't a manual - it's a companion on your journey to amplify the strengths of the educators you support.

The real work is just beginning, my friends. Aimee and Laurie are calling you to action, encouraging you to apply what you've learned, try new things, and remember that you're never alone. With a vibrant Personal Learning Network and a commitment to using data to drive progress, you'll be on your way to coaching excellence. By following these tips, you can become an effective coach who helps teachers grow and develop. Dive in, my fellow Sherpas, and let's navigate that rocky terrain together.

Chapter 1

Recruiting the Right Talent
~ Finding Skilled and Passionate Builders ~

"You have to go wholeheartedly into anything in order to achieve anything worth having."

—Frank Lloyd Wright (architect, designer, writer)

Helping others is truly invaluable. It is why we became educators, right? Those moments when the person you are helping smiles and says, "I get it!" or "Yes, that can work!" are why coaching, like teaching, can be so rewarding. As educators, we are curious and want to share our knowledge with our students.

If we were to place a bet, we guarantee that most of you got into the business of education because, at one point in your life or another, you either witnessed a spark of curiosity or ignited that spark, which in return gave someone else the power and knowledge to have learned something new. It is a fantastic feeling, isn't it? That ignition propelled the need to feel that feeling again. Welcome to coaching.

Naturally, we are passionate about the content of what we teach. We are bursting to share what we know with others. It gets us going every morning and makes our job seem less like work and more like a calling. This book is about harnessing those moments and creating opportunities for others to shine. It's about sharing your passion for helping others to develop their tool kit to be successful. Regardless of how you ended up in coaching—or are planning your journey into coaching—it is probably one of the most influential careers you can have.

As a teacher, you are almost held in the same regard as a TikTok influencer, spreading your love and passion beyond the four walls of your classroom. You are being invited, or will be asked, to share your knowledge and expertise with dozens of teachers and hundreds of students. Imagine how many sparks of curiosity you can create in one career.

Educators and trainers can use this book for any educational coaching scenario. We will primarily focus on educational technology because we have the most experience in the field; however, many protocols and practices can be translated into any type of coaching. You will hear from both of us about our experiences on all parts of the coaching cycle. We will share our wins and failures so you can learn what works best for you. It will be an honest conversation, and hopefully you can laugh along the way at our funniest moments and learn from our mistakes.

Before we dive in, we want to introduce ourselves. Hold on to your seats …

Laurie's Journey Into Coaching

In my first book, "SMILE Learning," I talk about my education journey and how I started using educational technology in the classroom. The book outlines how, when, and why to use educational technology with students using the SMILE method. As a frame of reference if you haven't read the book, SMILE is an acronym that helps you use technology with intentionality. Here is the basic outline:

S *Shine: Use technology to highlight your students' strengths.*
M *Motivate: Use technology to see failure as an opportunity to grow.*
I *Inspire: Use technology to inspire students to see their potential.*
L *Learn: Use technology to learn new things.*
E *Elephants: Use educational technology to overcome obstacles and find ways to work in harmony with other constraints. This strategy sets the foundation for leveraging the power of educational technology.*

In that book, I explain in detail why technology in the classroom is super important to me. I describe my conviction that technology plays a vital role in how we learn. In this book, we will explore how to be successful EdTech coaches. I had a very different journey than most to get to this point.

My first real job after getting a master's in teaching was at an insurance company. For the seven years I worked there, I constantly found myself in mentoring and coaching roles. I trained many new employees on everything from using Excel and writing estimates to dictating letters and training office staff. The job was evolving, but one thing stayed the same: I was helping my peers be successful in their careers. I wanted to give them the support they needed to do their job well. My measurement for success came from them being successful. I liked that feeling but found the content I was training on dull.

Once I had my children, I was frustrated with how often I was on the road training and how little time I was home with my family. I left insurance behind and opened a home-based daycare. I stayed home with my kids for three years, raising them and a few neighborhood children.

During that time, I started creating activities to help them all learn. We sang songs, did art projects, and explored imaginary play while the kids learned to count and identify letters. I loved reading stories with them and seeing their interests come to life. I loved the moments when they spoke their first words, read their first words, and figured things out on their own. I knew I wanted to teach, but it seemed impossible after so much time.

I took a chance and started subbing when my youngest was 3 ... and it changed my life. It was 11 years from the time I earned my master's in teaching to getting my first teaching job. While I took a long way to get here, I know this is where I belong. However, working as a professional development (PD) provider for an insurance company and running a home-based daycare gave me a unique perspective on training others. The PD I did at the insurance company was based on the art of selling, hiring, and training on insurance products.

While the topics were different, it gave me the opportunity to learn how adults learn best and how to structure the learning for all participants. It also shaped how I taught in my classroom. I don't have a traditional path that led me here. Instead, I can pull from my experiences to help others be successful, which brings me great joy.

My current role is as the Lead Coordinator for Instructional Technology Programs. Since beginning my career, I have been a sixth-grade teacher, a technology integration specialist, a Model Schools Coordinator, an adjunct professor, and an independent consultant. In each of these roles, I have learned more about how to support educators and students in succeeding in their goals. It also has given me a perspective unique in that I have been in every classroom at every grade level for over 17 years.

I have spent my entire career supporting adults and children alike. I love spending time in classrooms teaching students and modeling how to use technology effectively in the classroom. I also love supporting educators in whatever their goals are. Empowering educators to achieve their unique objectives is a passion of mine. I still create lessons and activities for all grade levels.

My focus for the past five years has been on our New York State Education computer science and digital fluency standards and integrating these standards using Universal Design for Learning, inquiry, and project-based learning. Still, as we go through this book, you will see in our examples that I've taught nearly every subject and have explored cross-curricular activities that will motivate students because of the real-life connections. I love using robots to introduce topics and have been training educators globally on educational technology for many years. I am excited that you are taking this journey with us. We are here to support you!

Aimee's Path to Empowerment Through Coaching

Believe it or not, I began my career as an art teacher—or a "struggling art teacher," as I like to describe it. What a time to enter education, and as an art educator, nonetheless. This was the early 2000s when most of the area was flooded with education majors.

Desperate to find a job to use my degree, I responded to an ad at a local, poor private school that advertised "PreK through eighth-grade art and computer teacher." Computer teacher? I mean, I was going for my master's in Educational Computing because I was trying to stand out from the rest ... fine, I'll apply.

First, let me give you a little backstory. I went to school for art. At one point in my high school career, I went to a career and technical school for a half day for its advertising and design program, but I left the program after my junior year because I felt it was too disciplined and technical. And get this—they wanted me to use the computer to create art. Forget. That. I knew how to code and use the computer, but they wanted me to combine my love for oil paints and pastels with an Apple iMac. Nah, I'm good.

Boy, was I wrong.

I ended up being offered the job at a poor, private school, and I took it, too. As I began my career as an art and computer teacher, I discovered two things about myself: my passion for creating a curriculum using technology and blending the content with creative, authentic lessons, and the fact that I had a natural knack for working with adults. Who knew? After a year of employment at St. Josaphat School, my principal approached me and said, "If you can teach art, you can teach computers. If you can teach computers to kids, you can teach adults."

I then became their official-unofficial tech coach, working with teachers in the one-computer classroom and getting them to sign up for my high-end eMachines Lab, where I networked the computers together to save on grading. Sadly, the school closed a year later, and I found myself looking for a job again, this time in computer education.

I will forever be grateful for the opportunity to have worked at that poor, private school as my first "real" teaching job. It not only gave me the experience that I sought after, but it also allowed me to discover that my love wasn't so much for art, but creativity. I also discovered a passion for transforming teaching using technology. I like to tell others that because of this experience, my career chose me.

Like Laurie, my road wasn't an entirely clear path as I had taken a few "breaks" from the classroom while raising children. But I didn't lie dormant and used this time wisely. My time at home with my children was valuable, as I had the opportunity to teach them how to read and write through play and creative projects to introduce them to sounds and letter recognition. I even had a well-known mom blog highlighting my adventures in teaching my children, which I had taken down a few years ago for personal reasons.

I also started my consulting business assisting local private schools, helping them integrate technology and developing their school websites. I adored the opportunities to work with multiple schools to meet educational technology needs while growing my craft and learning about the different needs of incorporating technology into the classroom.

Throughout my career, I have also learned that often, individuals will see talents or skill sets in you that you either overlook or don't believe in yourself enough for it to be true. I am forever grateful for the voices of encouragement and the opportunities I have had because others have believed in me. In my collective years in education, I have been in the classroom, subbing all content areas and grade levels, teaching art and computer science/digital literacy. I have been an educational technology coach, an assistant principal, a professional development specialist, and a supervisor.

When I ultimately decided to leave the classroom about seven years ago to continue to grow as an individual, I knew I wanted and was ready for that next step. This time, I wanted to focus my efforts on developing the art of leadership and simultaneously went back to school for my second master's degree in Educational Leadership. During this time, I also shifted my experience from the private sector of education to public education.

I also cannot speak enough about taking chances, stepping outside your comfort zone, and taking risks. You may have heard the saying "If it excites you and scares you at the same time, it probably means you should do it" from Cindi Madsen. Please do. You will grow and learn from those experiences more than staying in your lane, even if you fail. I will never regret the numerous professional failures I have had. Aside from great storytelling, they are a piece of who I am today.

I decided to step out of the classroom and into the world of coaching because I wanted to be able to magnify my passion for creating meaningful learning opportunities beyond the lives of the students that I saw every day and into the lives of many; even beyond what I can see in front of me. I am now a supervisor of instructional technology for a large district here in New York, overseeing instructional technology coaches and sharing my knowledge, skills, failures, passion, laughter, and everything in between. And now, I can share them with you. We are so excited to have you here and learn with you.

Let's jump in!

This Book's Blueprint

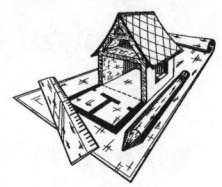

"The mind is like a parachute. It doesn't work if it is not open."
—Frank Zappa (musician, composer, and filmmaker)

Before we begin, though, let's talk about the book's structure. We hope that this book is one you come back to often. We hope that you will use it to structure your own coaching experiences and gain access to ideas that will enrich the experience for all. Sometimes we'll encourage you to reflect on your experiences and try something outside your comfort zone to stretch your practice. We encourage you to have a growth mindset that will hopefully stretch your thinking and abilities. But, most importantly, we want you to focus on your strengths and consider what you bring to the table.

What you think is no big deal might be something others struggle with. There could be something that you shine at that you don't even realize is extraordinary. Regardless of where you are in your career, as we begin this journey together, take some time to jot down your top five strengths. Then, if you are already a coach, ask others what they think you are good at. If you are not a coach, ask a peer what they identify as your strengths. Often, people see strengths in us that we overlook. You might be surprised at their answers.

We also hope this book helps those looking to help others in their learning journey. We will define all the roles that coaching can encompass as we go through this book, but for now, consider that this book is written for you if you support your peers in any way. This form of support can come in many ways: an afternoon PD session, a one-on-one exploration, a team that gets together to create a curriculum —really, anyone! You will find this book encompasses all educational institutions' roles. And you will find value in this book if you wear more than one hat!

Here are our objectives and what we hope to achieve:

🎯 Empower Educators

The primary goal of our book is to empower educators, such as yourself, with the knowledge, skills, and confidence to integrate technology into your teaching practices effectively to enable you to enhance student learning experiences and outcomes.

🎯 Facilitate Professional Growth

We, Aimee and Laurie, offer various examples of opportunities for ongoing professional growth and development in educational technology. This resource should help you. We hope that you return to it for guidance and inspiration as you evolve in your practice.

🎯 Promote Innovation and Creativity

In this book's chapters, we encourage you to embrace innovation and creativity in your teaching approaches by exploring new technologies and pedagogical strategies. We hope to foster a mindset of experimentation and a willingness to try new things in the classroom, even if you fail.

🎯 Cultivate a Collaborative Community

This book should encourage you to foster a sense of community among educators who are passionate about educational technology. We look to promote collaboration, knowledge sharing, and peer support to enhance collective learning and problem-solving.

Measure Impact and Effectiveness

Equally as important, this book should help establish mechanisms for measuring the impact and effectiveness of your technology integration efforts. We will share ways to collect data, assess outcomes, and continuously refine their practices based on evidence-based research and feedback.

 ## Address Educational Equity

Coaching often lets us see the big picture. Through the coaching lens, we will examine how you can recognize and address disparities in access to technology and digital resources among students and schools within your district or even classroom to classroom. We will also provide strategies for mitigating these inequities and ensuring all students have equal opportunities to benefit from technology-enhanced learning experiences.

 ## Promoting (and Practicing) Balance and Healthy Technology Use

Let's face it—we live in a connected world. As coaches, we are responsible for educating educators about balancing technology use and offline activities to promote overall well-being. We will also provide strategies for setting healthy boundaries and managing screen time effectively for you and the individuals you are coaching!

 ## Promote Responsible Digital Citizenship

Finally, we need to instill a sense of responsibility and ethics in ourselves, fellow educators, and students regarding the use of technology in everything we do. Throughout this book, we encourage thoughtful reflection on digital literacy, online safety, privacy, and digital citizenship.

What Should You Do?

So, you've picked up this book, and that's pretty amazing. Maybe you took a moment to analyze the cover. Or perhaps you looked at the final remark and the table of contents and skimmed through the many supplementary materials accompanying this book. Now what? Whether you volunteered or were voluntold to read this book, it will serve multiple purposes.

This book will help support and guide you whether you are starting your journey as a coach or have been in the field for a while and are looking to fine-tune your skills or different approaches to support. This book will help you navigate the field with proven instructional strategies, practical advice, and real-life examples. We have also included additional resources to support you in your role as an educational technology coach (ETC).

Suggestions if you are working through this book independently:

 ## Have an Open Mindset

When you dive into the book, approach it with an open mind and a curious spirit. Be willing to explore new ideas. However, this is your journey as a coach, so embrace the experience and have fun!

Take Notes and Explore the Resources

We recommend you utilize the available resources and digital documents and jot down concepts, ideas, and reflections as you read each chapter. Take time to engage actively by completing exercises, trying recommended practices, and reflecting on how the concepts apply to your coaching role.

Set Goals

Having a vision is vital for growth. As you read this book, we'll help you define specific learning objectives or goals you want to achieve by the end. We dedicated a whole chapter to this!

Apply What You Learn

Regardless of your career stage, utilize the knowledge and strategies from the book in real-world coaching scenarios. Reflect on the outcomes and adjust your approach as needed for continuous improvement. Reflect often.

If you read this book as part of a group, a professional learning network (PLN), or a book study, please follow the advice above. We also recommend the following:

Schedule Regular Meetings

Set a consistent schedule for group meetings to discuss each chapter or section of the book. Depending on your pace, you can have weekly, biweekly, or monthly meetings.

Establish Clear Objectives

Define the book study's goals and objectives. Consider what specific skills or knowledge you hope participants will gain individually and as a group.

💡 Encourage Active Participation

Rotate your participants' roles for each meeting, such as discussion leader, note-taker, timekeeper, or activity facilitator. This can keep meetings dynamic and engaging.

💡 Facilitate Discussions

During meetings, facilitate meaningful discussions by asking open-ended questions, encouraging diverse perspectives, and relating the book's content to real-world experiences. Create opportunities for participants to share insights, challenges, and success stories associated with implementing the book's strategies in their coaching or teaching roles.

ArchiTech
Book Study
Reflection
Questions

You can also use our chapter reflection questions for a book study; you can access them by scanning the QR code to the left. Feel free to make a copy of this resource.

💡 Celebrate Achievements

Celebrate achievements and milestones reached during the book study, such as completing a section or implementing a new coaching strategy. When appropriate, tag along on a coaching cycle to share and join one another on the journey.

Whether you conquer this book solo or have a group to champion you on your way, you will ultimately find that this book is written in various ways. Please start where you find it more purposeful. More importantly, please share your knowledge, learnings, and everything else as you embark on your journey with us at @SMILELearning (Laurie) and @AJBloom2pnt0 (Aimee).

Earlier, we mentioned focusing on your strengths as you explore coaching throughout this book. We wanted to take a moment and discuss a bit more what we mean by this. In schools, we collect data to look for weaknesses and areas where growth is needed. But, in the so-called "real world," your strengths can bring you success and satisfaction in your job. It is the strengths that you need to lean into as you explore EdTech coaching. And it is definitely something you want to explore as you coach. Finding the strengths in others and allowing them to shine and grow will be a task worth doing.

 **Laurie**

If you need help thinking about your strengths, there are some places to learn about yourself. I was one of those people who believed that strengths meant you were good at school, sports, art, or music. It never occurred to me that there are other things to be good at. Then, while in college, I took a course on career exploration and was required to read "What Color is Your Parachute?" by Richard Nelson Bolles. The book helps you explore your passions, your inner feelings about all aspects of life, and what you like to do. It kept coming up that I was a creative. I remember being so frustrated because I was far from artistic. I had so many art failures that I assumed there was no way I could do a creative job. I didn't realize that being artistic and being creative are incredibly different.

I remember feeling like a failure and thinking no job would be fulfilling. Fast-forward to my first real job at an insurance firm when my boss handed me a book called "Now, Discover Your Strengths" by Donald O. Clifton and Marcus Buckingham. It was pivotal to me at that moment, and I realized I was tackling my job life wrong and was definitely in the wrong field.

It's not about being good or bad at something, anyway. It's about using the skills already inside of you as a gift and applying them to what you are doing. EdTech allows for a ton of creativity. Teaching does, too! Every day, we must create *learning experiences for our students, activities that engage and excite our students to want to learn. How you accomplish this relies on your ability to use your strengths to support student learning.*

Aimee

When I think of the word "strength," I envision someone who has overcome tough times to achieve their goals and aspirations. Over the years, I've understood that strength has many layers. I used to jokingly compare my life to an onion, with many, many layers. While some may initially view this metaphor as unfavorable because onions can be pungent and make your eyes water when you cut them, the strength and the rich antioxidants found in each layer are often overlooked. Each layer is a protective barrier for the onion's core, much like the core of who you are.

Then I discovered that the onion metaphor is more than just a figure of speech—it's a real thing used all the time. At first, I was ready to rebel and forfeit using the metaphor, like I usually do when something becomes a social norm. But you know what? I've come to embrace it.

What makes you strong or good at something? Strength is a matter of perspective. I often reflect on this: Is strength your natural ability that makes you feel strong at something, or is it the fact that you showed up in the first place to give it a try?

I will piggyback off a topic Laurie shared with you earlier—one that we discussed because, oddly, it is a commonality between us: creativity.

Unlike Laurie, I have always considered myself to be a very creative person. When I was young, I loved writing books, creating characters, and inventing new games. Was I artistic? Absolutely. It was a strength of mine. In high school, I took nearly every art class, including an independent study course tailored just for me. I was considered to be a very talented artist in my high school. However, when I started college, I was surrounded by incredibly talented individuals in a sea of the best of the best. I felt that my strength, shared by others in my field of study, was measured against them instead of me competing against myself.

Nonetheless, when I started college, I wanted to try everything! Everything from fabric design and media design to painting and sculpture. Sculpture is a medium that I didn't have much experience with, and I could barely mold together a candy cane, let alone a 3D self-portrait, which, by the way, was my first major assignment in my sculpture class. Creating sculptures was a weakness of mine.

The situation was made worse because we spent much time creating spheres and cones in our in-person class. Simple, right? As homework, we were tasked with sculpting a self-portrait using 30 pounds of clay. We were left on our own with minimal support.

It was about halfway through the semester when we were asked to lug our 30-pound clay head pieces into the school for a peer and professor critique. I don't know whose self-portrait I was carrying. However, I showed up for the process. I was among the last students to be critiqued—eager, nervous, and scared. I knew that sculpture was not my strength. Although I brought a clay head that day, I am unsure whose head it was.

I innocently placed my 30-pound head on the stool in the middle of the class as my professor walked around, shaking his head with a disgusted look on his face. He took a 2x4 and slammed my head in. For clarification, that's the clay head, not my head.

After he smashed my head down to a pile of mush, he looked at me and said, "You need to start over again."

I left carrying my 30-pound pile of mush, feeling defeated. I thought I would never be good at sculpture or anything else I had never tried before because everybody else was much better than I was. I was trapped in my thoughts.

I didn't return to class for about a week or two. One day, I woke up and said, "You know, today's going to be the day that I go back to class. And I'm going to be the best sculpture student ever!"

Now, I knew that I would never be the best sculpture student ever, but what I did learn about myself are my true strengths. Number one is my perseverance. Some call it stubbornness, but I prefer perseverance—it has a better ring to it. Despite my immense embarrassment and overwhelming fear that I was not going to succeed, I still persevered, and I showed up.

An Introduction to the Woo® CliftonStrengths Theme

The second thing that came from this experience is a characteristic I have always possessed but never thought of as a strength: my ability to make connections. According to Gallup's CliftonStrengths, a professional development opportunity provided to me years later when I was a technology integration specialist solidified this strength as my ability to WOO—Winning Others Over. (Check out Gallup's CliftonStrengths by scanning the QR code to the left.)

I learned everything there was to know about that sculpture professor. I learned the type of sculpture he did, where his exhibits were, and who his favorite artists were. My final bronze sculpture emulated everything I knew about this person.

I realized that my strength was not in sculpture but in creativity and my approach to achieving my goals. When I had to find innovative ways to succeed, I discovered the importance of perseverance and determination. Sometimes, you uncover your strengths during your weakest moments, so it's crucial to take that moment to recognize your strengths.

Artistic Ability vs. Creativity

This book will be filled with stories from Aimee and Laurie about our lives and journey into EdTech coaching. It will provide you opportunities to think about your abilities and your creative outlets as you read the following stories. Why does this matter in a book all about EdTech coaching? Well, each of the people that you support and coach will have their feelings and frustrations. They will have their own biases around what they think they do well and what they have anxiety over.

For me (Laurie), creativity was a hurdle to overcome my bias. For me (Aimee), it was a clear path that made me a better coach. Take a moment and reflect on the moments that made you feel you were good—or not good—at something. This is an important part of the process.

 **Laurie**

When I was young, I loved to draw. I would doodle all day in my coloring books and on my easel chalkboard. I loved taking a blank white page and seeing the images I saw in my brain come to life on the page. I never thought of myself as good or bad at drawing. I was hoping that with practice, I would get better. Then, in the third grade, my art teacher crushed my love for drawing. I started at a new school and drew her a picture early that year. I was so proud of the hills with a sun

peeking out and all the colorful flowers I drew on the page. I couldn't wait to hear her react over the time I took to make her something. When I got to art class, I handed her the drawing with a huge smile. Imagine my horror when she proclaimed that what I drew was not art. She tore the picture in half, threw it in the trash, and told me to sit back down. From then on, I felt anxious whenever I was asked to draw anything. I stopped drawing entirely and added art and creativity into the "Laurie is not good at this" category. I still get heart palpitations when asked to draw something; it is something I still struggle with and probably always will.

It never occurred to me that "artistic" and "creative" were completely different things. It wasn't until tools like Canva and Buncee were available that my thoughts on this changed. Technology opened so many creative doors for me and helped me see that I am incredibly creative—always have been. It was just breaking down the barriers between my natural talent and the tech world that could shift that understanding. So, instead of focusing on what I can't do artistically, I look for tools to remove that barrier and fulfill my creative bucket.

 **Aimee**

As I mentioned above, I am artistic. For as long as I can remember, I have loved creating art. Like Laurie, I would spend hours drawing and painting. My step-grandfather and mother were also highly artistic and possessed way more talent than I ever did, teaching me everything that I knew at a very young age. No matter how passionately creative I was and much I loved to create, once I graduated from the second grade and moved on to intermediate school, art was my least favorite subject.

Why? Wonderful question. This is where creativity disrupts artistic ability.

In second grade, my art teacher was a TAB teacher (Teaching for Artistic Behavior). This particular style of teaching leads students to find their passion in centers, learning about the materials through self-exploration. I loved it. I even had a painting I created on my own accord hanging in the Albright-Knox Art Gallery in Buffalo, New York. I was allowed to create the art that I was passionate about.

That all changed from third grade on and well into my college years. I was told what and how to create, and I was given cookie-cutter assignments that drove me insane. Did I do well in art? Well, yes. Of course! But it was 100% out of compliance, and a tiny part of me just wanted to show off more than I was excited about anything I created.

I'm still like this today. My creative side is way more powerful and dangerous if you simply allow me to exploit it. Please, do not tell me what to create. Give me a problem, and "Yo, I'll solve it." (Yes, I quoted Vanilla Ice.) Allow me to be passionately creative. Thank you.

It's important to remember that every individual possesses a unique capacity for creativity, including Laurie. Creativity is an inherent part of human nature. Many of you may be able to relate to our stories above. Perhaps you were one of those who would proudly boast, "I'm not creative. I couldn't draw a stick figure to save my life!"

Was this creative self-doubt your harsh reflection on your perceived lack of artistic ability? Was it an onlooker judgment call? Perhaps you simply weren't given many opportunities to be creative in your formative years? As the esteemed Sir Ken Robinson once fervently expressed, "We are educating people out of their creative capacities … I believe this passionately, that we don't grow into creativity, we grow

Why schools need to embrace kids' creativity
Sir Ken Robinson

out of it. Or rather, we get educated out of it." Please take a moment to watch his Ted Talk on creativity and schools, entitled "Why Schools Need to Embrace Kids' Creativity," by scanning the QR code to the left.

Artistic ability allows artists to possess the skills to paint, poets to write, and musicians to play music. While artistic expression is a well-known form of creativity, it's essential to recognize that creativity extends far beyond this. It encompasses generating innovative ideas, solving complex problems, and thinking unconventionally. This requires both divergent and convergent thinking, abductive reasoning, and the skill of visualization. Creativity and creative thinking are becoming more recognized as essential, even to the point that the 2023 World Economic Forum identified creativity as one of the most highly sought-after skills in today's modern world (scan the World Economic Forum QR code for more information).

World Economic Forum | Future of Jobs 2023

With this in mind, we need to create instances in our training for educators, classrooms, and personal lives to exercise our creative brains. Many resources are at our fingertips to assist us in purposefully planning episodes of creative thinking into our prescribed curriculum or created workshops and training material. One of those resources is using generative AI tools that can help you in this endeavor.

Regarding exercising your creative brain, take a moment to look at Adobe's "10 Exercises to Spark Original Thinking and Increase Creativity" by scanning the QR code to expand and exercise your creative mind. Think: When was the last time you were able to be creative? How do you include creativity in your professional life?

Adobe Express
10 Exercises to Spark Original Thinking & Increase Creativity

AI and Its Use in Writing This Book

As we embark on this journey, we must disclose that we have utilized artificial intelligence to create this book. We have distinct viewpoints regarding generative AI and its role in writing, as well as very similar ones. Still, our acknowledgments will provide consistent and thorough explanations of its involvement in how we used it individually and collectively in our writings.

 Aimee

I ramble a lot when I tell stories. Knowing this, when I tell stories throughout this book, please know that I first use speech-to-text to capture my thoughts quickly and honestly. They are often wordy and rarely right to the point. When I have my "rough draft" created, I run it through Grammarly's AI to make it more coherent and focused while sounding like me. Yes, I go back in and add edits to ensure my story still captures the true essence of Aimee. It's very similar to what I did here.

This part goes without saying: I use generative AI to help me with my grammar and sentence structure and ensure that what I am saying is coherent. Often, I explain something through text that makes sense only to me. The "improve it" feature in generative AI allowed me to compare and contrast how I wanted to convey a message in various ways. It also allowed me to reword and make more sense of my explanations.

Collectively, we used generative AI to help us define and identify any missing gaps in the topics we wanted to explore. When we first assembled the book, we ran our notes through the generative AI tool Gemini to ask us to identify any topics we could have been missing, thus providing us with topics we perhaps had overlooked. Finally, we used generative AI to help us come up with this book's title and each chapter's title. We kept challenging Gemini to create titles with which we were satisfied—or parts of titles that we smashed together until we were 100% satisfied.

 **Laurie**

Artificial intelligence is the buzzword at every conference, meeting, webinar, and social media post about education. I was fortunate to be in the first cohort offered about AI that was cohosted by ISTE (the International Society for Technology in Education), which offers resources, conferences, and frameworks to help educators effectively integrate technology, and GM (General Motors), which supports educators in learning about artificial intelligence in the classroom, to showcase how AI is used in industry. We were looking at whether there were any applications within education at that time, and it was eye-opening what AI could do for education. Even before ChatGPT, this highlighted the need for me to explore emerging technologies regularly.

For this book, I used AI in several ways. The biggest one was using Grammarly to fix my grammar. While I was an English teacher for many years, I still tend to be comma happy! Plus, sometimes what I have in my mind doesn't always translate well onto paper, and using AI can help me organize my thoughts. I also used AI with Aimee to create titles and explore topics. It helped organize ideas for me and sometimes caught an area I missed when writing from my brain alone. By no means did this supersede either of us writing this book. Instead, it was a guide on the side, a tutor, and often a reminder of what was needed to convey our thoughts and ideas. When harnessed correctly, AI can support your work, but you still need to do the work!

I asked Gemini its thoughts; here is its response. (Note: I love asking Gemini to be sassy, so I asked it here, too, to keep it light and fun!)

Prompt: Give me a sassy answer about why and when to use AI to improve writing. Keep it to a top five.

 **Top 5 Reasons to Use AI for Writing (or, Why Your Words Don't Need a Human Touch)**

1. *Who needs a thesaurus when you have a robot? AI can suggest words you never knew existed, making your writing sound like you're a linguistic genius.*
2. *Writer's block? AI can spit out a whole paragraph faster than you can say "I'm stuck." It's like having a bottomless well of ideas, minus the existential crisis.*
3. *Grammar is for nerds. AI can catch those pesky errors that even your English teacher missed. So, go ahead, make mistakes, it's what AI is for.*
4. *Need a second opinion? AI can tell you if your writing is too boring, dramatic, or weird. It's like having a brutally honest friend who doesn't care about your feelings.*
5. *Who needs a human touch? AI can write in any style, tone, or voice you want. So, whether you're going for formal, informal, or straight-up sassy, AI has got you covered.*

***

I promise you that I am still a word nerd, but even I need help sometimes! Ask any AI tool to help you with anything in this book for which you need more support. You may find the answers to be helpful!

Remember that AI isn't perfect. While it has been around for over 70 years, the way we use it today is still in its infancy. Check for errors, bias, inaccuracies, or plain old hallucinations.

But what are hallucinations in AI?

Hallucinations can occur in many ways when using artificial intelligence. We asked Gemini, which is Google's generative AI tool, to define it for us. This was its response:

In the context of artificial intelligence, "hallucination" refers to the phenomenon where an AI model generates incorrect or misleading information. This can manifest in various ways, such as:

- *Factually incorrect statements: The AI might produce text or generate images that contain false or misleading information.*
- *Invented information: The AI might fabricate information that doesn't exist in its training data or the real world.*
- *Misinterpretation of prompts: The AI might misunderstand user prompts, leading to irrelevant or nonsensical outputs.*

AI hallucinations can arise due to several factors, including:

- *Insufficient training data: If the AI model is trained on a limited dataset, it may lack the necessary information to generate accurate responses.*
- *Incorrect assumptions: The AI might make incorrect assumptions about the world or the user's intent, leading to inaccurate or irrelevant outputs.*
- *Biases in training data: If the training data contains biases, the AI model may replicate those biases in its outputs.*

It's important to be aware of AI hallucinations and to critically evaluate the information generated by AI models. As AI technology continues to advance, it's crucial to develop techniques to mitigate and prevent AI hallucinations.

Laurie has a recent video about AI ethics; you can check it out by scanning the QR code to the right.

Laurie Guyon's
Guardian of ai Ethics
YouTube video

As we embark on this journey together, we invite you to embrace coaching as a catalyst for educational transformation. You are the right talent. You desire to share your expertise with those you work with and beyond. This book will give you a solid foundation for building and thriving within our coaching community. Remember that coaching is not just about your knowledge. It is about inspiring growth, fostering innovation, and empowering educators to reach beyond what they thought was possible. Let's work together to create a future where every educator feels supported, valued, and equipped to make a lasting impact on student learning.

Chapter 2

Defining the EdTech Coach's Role
~ Architect, Builder, and Guide ~

"A profound design process eventually makes the patron, the architect, and every occasional visitor in the building a slightly better human being."

—**Juhani Pallasmaa** (architect, author, and architectural theorist)

What Is a Coach?

When we think about coaching, we may have different ideas. For some, a coach may lead or, most likely, cheer you on. A coach can lead in many ways, and you may jump from one role to another anytime. In this chapter, we will break down all the roles you may have as a coach. Sometimes, you may be a bit of all of them, while in some instances, you must foster just one of these essential roles.

To be a successful coach, you will wear many hats. We outline the big ones here, but with your skill set, you have others that are just as important for success. Reflect on your coaching experiences, if you have had some, and see where your strengths shine. Suppose you find areas where you need to foster growth and take some time to learn more from this book. You should grab a highlighter and a pen to jot down your thoughts as you explore the roles.

 **Laurie**

My first thought when I hear the word "coach" is someone in charge of a sports team. If you think about your earliest coaches, they were for some little league or whatever sport you played. You already know I'm not an artist, but I'm an even worse athlete. Somehow, though, I was part of many athletic teams growing up. And while I was terrible on the field or the court, coaches always encouraged me to take on a role that allowed me to be a part of the team. For example, my softball and field hockey coaches asked me to be a scorekeeper in middle school.

If you are an athlete, you probably laughed at that, but I was so inept on the field that they found a way to keep me as part of the experience. This allowed me to at least practice with the team. For some, this might have seemed like a kick in the gut, but I just wanted to belong on a team. Coaches saw that I was happy to be the cheerleader for others and offered me that role often.

In high school, I made the JV volleyball team in 10th grade. In 11th grade, the varsity coach told me I would never make varsity, but he had a role for me anyway. That year, they didn't have a JV coach. He asked me to be the "coach" of that JV team, help with practices, and sit on the bench at the varsity games as an assistant. I gladly said yes. I wanted to be with my friends, and I loved that I could help the team, even if it was on the sidelines. It was a unique experience that opened future doors that I never dreamed possible.

Fast-forward to my teaching years, and my friend, who coached the varsity volleyball team and had been a Division 1 player herself, asked me to be the JV coach. I told her I had little knowledge of the game and that I had never made a varsity sport, but she wouldn't hear of it. She said she could help me learn. On my first day as coach, I was terrible. The girls were frustrated with my lack of experience, and I had to find a way to get them to trust me. Thankfully, YouTube can teach you anything. I watched videos, listened to other coaches, and took notes on different drills to help the girls.

During the last day of tryouts, I got my first win. We required all of the players to run a mile on the track. The girls groaned and complained that they didn't see the point. I told them I would run it with them. About halfway through the mile, a few girls were struggling. I slowed and ran right next to them, encouraging them and letting them know I wouldn't leave them behind. We all crossed the finish line together and cheered each other on. One of the more experienced players approached me and said I gained her respect because I was willing to run with the girls and encourage them as I ran. She said I still had much to learn, but she knew I was at least putting in the effort.

While I will talk a lot about tools and technology integration, coaching is about helping each other cross that finish line together. It is about assisting others to see their potential and letting them know they are not alone. That is what a coach does, and it's a vital part of what I do when I facilitate any training, support every teacher, and help others learn with me.

Aimee

You know what's weird? I never considered myself a coach. To me, a coach was someone who was always up in your grill, yelling as a way of "motivating" you to succeed. At least, that's what's always portrayed in movies and shows.

I never participated in organized sports. So when I was asked to assist teachers with their use of technology in my mid-twenties, having only one solid year of "real" teaching under my belt (I say "real" because I spent a few years teaching three- and four-year-olds how to use the computer at a day care), the word "coach" never came to mind. What I was back then, assisting teachers in the one-computer classroom, helped shape me into who I am now: your champion.

Since I never participated in organized sports and despised being "told" what to create, I am sure this next thought will shock you: I never liked titles. And let me tell you, I have had my share of them—Specialist and Coordinator being two of my favorites. Oddly enough, I never officially held the "coach" title. So, titles aside, my role was essentially the same: guiding and championing change, supporting others and being a thought partner. So, if I am to define the term "coach" for the purposes of writing this book, the latter would be it. I like one of the titles that Gemini suggested, which is The Catalyst of Classroom Cool.

If coaching is the topic, and we were to mind map words that relate to coaching, we would use terms like facilitator, collaborator, or coordinator. Not everyone learns in the same way, and there are many ways to be in a coaching role. Let's explore some of the more common roles and how they're essential to coaching.

Core Pillars

Facilitator

Keith Hughes (@hiphughes), an educator friend from Buffalo, New York, once posted that he is a FOLE—a Facilitator of the Learning Experience. He said that "teacher" sounds as if we have all the answers and must give all the information. But as a facilitator, we help others find the answers. We want to help others learn, and we don't want to be the ones doing all the talking.

Think about how you learn best. Is it through a lecture where you take notes and listen, or is it when something is more hands-on, and you can figure things out independently with guidance? Do you prefer to ask questions upfront, or are you one to listen and then ask questions at the end? Remember that no matter how you prefer to teach and coach, you must consider the needs of those you teach and coach—these may vary incredibly.

In the facilitating role, we support the work of others. The bulk of the work is done by the people being coached. We offer guidance, resources, and support. We strive to help others find answers and determine the best path for them to learn. A learning process facilitator offers others the opportunity to have agency over their learning.

A facilitator focuses on encouraging others to find the answers. Facilitators build confidence and help educators explore independently to enhance their professional development. While this type of coaching is guided, it often lends itself to more of a sideline supporter versus being in the trenches with the educators. Facilitators encourage collaboration, model expectations, and provide feedback to help the learning journey. What a facilitator *won't* do is tell others what to do but rather work alongside them to support their objectives.

This type of coaching is well suited to self-motivated people with a strong growth mindset. It can also lead to a culture shift in which innovation and advocacy are encouraged and rewarded. This can be pivotal in transforming educational practices and creating an environment that values continuous improvement.

Many teachers want their students to be explorers, critical thinkers, and problem solvers. If we want that in our classrooms, we should strive for it in our training. By modeling the facilitator role, you will help educators reflect on what they found valuable in that practice and bring it back to the classroom for their students.

Collaborator

In the role of collaborator, the coach works alongside educators to help with the goals they set together. This can enhance the outcomes by promoting continuous improvement and lending itself to innovative ideas. The collaborator role differs from a facilitator's as the learning happens in tandem. A facilitator will guide, but a collaborator will partner. This is the first step for those dipping their toes into coaching, as they can hone their skills and learn from those they are coaching.

One of the most significant aspects of collaboration is the ability to build a team. If a collaborator and an educator must complete something together or have similar goals, this type of coaching works well. Establishing shared objectives helps enhance relationships and foster connections and trust.

This coaching method is ideal for individuals engaged in professional learning. Collaborating with peers ensures that PD is customized to fit the group's needs. It allows exploration, curriculum alignment, and assessment to be firmly placed in the coaching cycles. While facilitators encourage innovation, collaborators engage in that innovative practice and adjust the coaching styles to fit the needs of those they are coaching.

Think of the collaborator's role as building a community. Within this coaching strategy, participants are part of the educational ecosystem that allows collaboration with the team to transform learning and the use of technology.

Connector

While facilitators have the guardrails and collaborators are team players, connectors ensure all moving parts come together. For example, a connector might introduce those they are coaching to a PLN, a like-minded peer, or even someone who can broaden the team's thinking. A connector will see the ripple forming and ensure everyone who needs to be inside the ripple is connected. This is also true for resources; a coach in a connector role loves to create and compile resources for others to use. They also keep up with the latest trends and tools that can be helpful to those they coach.

The connector values and facilitates professional networks. These can be cohort meetings, webinars, workshops, meetups, or conferences to share ideas, strategies, and experiences for a common goal. Connectors will also examine the big picture of what the team wants to accomplish and ensure all parties can sit at the table. A connector builds partnerships and considers all the stakeholders who can impact the outcome; the connector is the coach people turn to when there's a problem to solve or an idea that needs to be nurtured. The connector coach will know who needs to be linked up with whom and will facilitate a personalized connection with all parties.

Connectors are often problem solvers and doers, offering solutions based on needs, whereas facilitators guide others toward solutions. Since every person's needs differ, both roles can be incredibly valuable—and sometimes, a bit of both is needed.

Connectors, like collaborators, will personalize professional development based on needs. Connectors often bring others to host the PD based on expertise, while collaborators will be heavily involved in the training. One-to-one interactions may happen more often for connectors than for collaborators, as connectors try to connect dots one by one to make sure those being coached are getting what they need at the level they're currently at. Connectors will be among the best advocates for equitable access, identifying and addressing barriers within a team's goals, and helping find opportunities to meet the needs of all learners.

Connectors are less concerned with innovation. Instead, they build networks, share resources, create communication lines, and offer technology solutions to benefit all parties within a coaching cohort.

Coordinator

The word "coordinator" suggests a role similar to that of a connector, but a coordinator's work is often characterized by more organized thought and design. Coordinators must be detail-oriented and able to coordinate all the pieces to support others. They must also have vision and control over all the moving parts, with a clear focus on the end goal of the coaching.

Coordinators develop and communicate this vision and host regular check-ins to ensure the goals are achievable and that each initiative is being cultivated. Consider the coordinator a bridge between the end goal and the stakeholders. Coordinators know current practices and see where shifts and tweaks are possible. They offer a compelling vision for technology integration by connecting those they are coaching with the right products, tools, and resources to foster that success. They are instrumental in setting measurable goals (see SMART goals in chapter seven) that can be taken to reality.

Coaching has many complex and movable parts. The coordinator must understand the educational environments and then pair that with a deep understanding of technology and pedagogical trends to help their mentees evolve and be a catalytic force for innovation and improvement.

Coordinators know all stakeholders, have made partnerships and relationships between all parties, and have advocated for the right policies and guidelines within a district to cultivate these environments. A coordinator role is not often the first coaching role one has, but rather one developed over time. In a coordinator role, one knows the complexities of how our education systems work and has tried to find proper ways to overcome any obstacles. Often, the coordinator is one step beyond the boots-on-the-ground level of coaching and instead works with other coaches by encouraging innovation and experimentation for a common goal.

Advocate

Since the coordinator role is broader, the advocate role might be the first significant coaching role one takes on. Before becoming a connector or facilitator, one may have previously worn—or will eventually wear—the advocate hat. To picture it in motion, consider something you are passionate about. It could be an inquiry-based learning opportunity, the exploration of immersive technologies, or even the science of reading. An advocate thinks of ways to help others see the value and rewards of implementing the ideas, evaluating and testing their theories and learning all they can to encourage implementing these ideas. These ideas don't have to be revolutionary, but they can shift the possibilities and contribute to student achievement.

An advocate also supports and encourages others. They find ways to spotlight what another educator is doing by showcasing their process and learning and how it has increased engagement. They might highlight another educator's work in a faculty meeting, a newsletter, or in a grander way to a global audience. An advocate might recommend another educator for a new role, a department lead position, or an award to showcase their success

Advocates work on achieving the buy-in frequently required to take ideas further, showcasing their persuasive skills to the administration and presenting evidence-based practices and success stories to other educators. Advocates build that community by highlighting the value added to the ideas and skills of others. Additionally, advocates can offer professional learning to teachers to help others acquire the skills and confidence needed to integrate these new opportunities. At some point, the advocate can then shift to the connector or the facilitator role to bring together the resources, the policies, and the professional learning to spread the goodness to others.

Another important part of advocacy is that coaches need to consider how each tool or idea affects all populations, working to ensure equity and accessibility in all parts of education and promoting accessible technologies and practices for diverse needs.

Supporter/Confidant/Champion

Often, your role as a coach is to support your educators and be someone who listens. You could create the best workshop that you think will help foster a skill, but it can flop if you cannot adjust and listen to the group's needs.

 **Laurie**

I was working with a group of department heads at a school on implementing computer science into their curriculum. The training included learning about using artificial intelligence. I prepared a fun workshop on Padlet that included a

chance for participants to create their avatars using AI, explore the standards, and think of ways to align their curriculum to these standards.

If you have never heard of or used Padlet, you will find it to be a tool you can use for multiple purposes. At its basic level, it allows you to create a resource repository for anything in the classroom. You can use Padlet to share ideas, brainstorm, or even create AI-generated images. This bulletin board in your classroom allows your students to share video, audio, text, and images easily. (Scan the QR code to see a Padlet example and add in your own "I Can't Draw" image.) Similar to Padlet is Wakelet. Both of these tools offer free and premium levels.

Padlet example and add in your own "I Can't Draw"

The first activity engaged the group, but we hit a few roadblocks with passwords and access; some participants could do the task, but others could only watch. Then, I reviewed their curriculum map to help them identify areas where alignment needed support.

When I started to explain the next activity, where they were to look at ways to integrate the computer science standards into their core curriculum, the workshop went totally off the rails. I immediately switched from a facilitator role to a supporter and confidant, listening to their fears and concerns. They felt they didn't have enough training yet on the standards and lacked the knowledge of computer science to consider integrating it into their curriculum. We realized a vocabulary gap and needed to break down each standard to understand what it asked us to do. I knew we would not do what I had outlined for the rest of the workshop. Instead, I gathered their thoughts, listened to their concerns, and considered what I would do the next time we met.

When we met the next time, I thought I had prepared just what they needed. I created a series of vocabulary-rich activities to help them understand computer science and how it could look in each content area. However, I had failed to hear what it was they needed. Right off the bat, one teacher was upset that I hadn't aligned the activities with his business curriculum. I had an English teacher who wanted me to tell her what standards she was responsible for and would not engage in the activities without an explicit list. And yet another teacher expressed that he felt his time was being wasted and that no progress was being made.

Their administration was also in the room and agreed that we needed to reassess how these standards would be rolled out. But more importantly, we still needed to find ways to overcome the fear and frustration that the teachers felt over adding new standards to their already packed curriculum.

There was no easy answer in this scenario. As you reflect on your coaching experiences, both as the coach and the one being coached, how would you have handled this situation? What could I have done differently in your eyes to meet the needs of these educators? I sat back and allowed the teachers to discuss their fears and frustrations. I stopped offering solutions and let them air their concerns and grievances. The administrators in the room only pushed back when they felt it necessary, but they also just listened. Although only a little was accomplished to move forward on meeting the standards, the educators at least knew we were willing to listen.

A supporter knows when just to sit back and listen. Sharing best practices is valuable, but more often than not, a person being coached just needs someone to hear them. Supporters must listen to concerns and ideas to co-plan lessons and explore tools that support achievement. Sometimes, it's just about offering emotional support. It's known that integrating something new can be frustrating, that it may fail, and that stepping outside comfort zones can feel overwhelming. However, these concerns can be overcome with support, helping peers become more comfortable and proficient. As a supporter, the goals and skills to integrate are clear, but ensuring that those being coached are on the same page is essential.

Teachers should also feel secure when coming up with a discussion and concern. If they don't trust, shifting to connector and collaborator roles is essential to build relationships. One can't be all things at all times. Still, as a champion for them, opportunities can be offered to build on the relationship by listening and providing personalized support. Work on empowering those coached to take risks and explore new pedagogical or technological approaches. This empowerment will help those coached to grow, encouraging innovation and enhanced learning experiences.

Counselor

The final element of coaching is to be a counselor. A counselor encompasses the roles of supporter and facilitator, but it also includes so much more. As a counselor, the coach will help those being coached to adopt a growth mindset toward the topic, tool, or pedagogy being addressed. Counselors emphasize and develop the skills and understandings within the relationship journey. When in a counseling role, addressing the root cause of resistance or anxiety about shifting the practice around whatever is being coached on is possible. Through a lot of discourse and interventions, a counselor can help those they coach to meet their goals.

A counselor can play an essential role in the coaching process in many ways. Understanding the fears will help create a path the counselor and the educator can navigate together. Counselors can help manage emotions so the educator does not feel overwhelmed or inadequate. Think about a time when learning or understanding something was impossible. Working through it in smaller parts can overcome that fear, leading to success. A counselor will celebrate those small wins to help guide educators toward their goals.

A counselor guides educators toward a specific end goal, helping them reflect on the process and plan for the next steps. Additionally, counselors will help identify areas where professional learning can aid improvement. The small wins achieved through professional learning can significantly impact individuals, teams, and organizations. Learners can build confidence, momentum, and a sense of accomplishment by focusing on achievable, short-term goals. As a counselor, it is important to point out the impact of those small wins in practice—they can serve as building blocks for more significant and long-term achievements.

Counselors can play a crucial role in identifying areas where professional learning can be beneficial. Through assessments, discussions, and observations, a counselor can help individuals and teams recognize their strengths, weaknesses, and areas for improvement. They can then recommend specific learning opportunities and strategies that align with the learner's goals and objectives.

Once areas for improvement have been identified, the counselor can assist in developing and implementing a plan for professional learning. Upon identifying areas for growth, the counselor can facilitate the creation and execution of a comprehensive professional development strategy. This plan may include attending workshops, seminars, or online courses and reading books and articles, shadowing colleagues, or seeking mentorship opportunities. The plan could include participating in workshops, meetings, or online courses, reading relevant books and articles, shadowing colleagues, or finding mentorship opportunities. The counselor can provide guidance and support throughout the learning process, ensuring that the learner stays motivated and on track.

The impact of professional learning extends beyond the individual learner. When team members engage in professional learning, they can develop a shared understanding of best practices, strategies, and terminology. This can lead to improved communication, collaboration, and decision-making. Engaging in professional learning can cultivate a culture prioritizing continuous improvement and innovation within an organization, enhancing communication, collaboration, and decision-making processes.

The small wins achieved through professional learning can significantly impact individuals, teams, and organizations. By identifying areas for improvement, developing a learning plan, and providing guidance and support, a counselor can help learners achieve their goals and reach their full potential. This encouragement toward a continuous learning cycle can lead to incredible learning and growth.

Like a supporter, a counselor will work on improving relationships between all parts of the community in school and beyond to create a supportive environment. It's about breaking down the silos and finding a professional learning network where open communication can flourish, and innovative culture can be fostered.

Imagine breaking down barriers and joining a professional learning network that promotes open dialogue and encourages creativity. Educational coaching goes beyond the mere transfer of knowledge and skills. Counselors are pivotal in guiding and supporting educators as they embrace and incorporate new tools, teaching methods, and technologies into their practices. They help educators comprehend the rationale behind their actions, alleviate apprehensions and anxieties, and cultivate a nurturing environment for professional growth.

By recognizing incremental progress and celebrating achievements, counselors instill confidence and momentum in educators, propelling them toward continuous improvement. Effective educational coaching fosters a culture that embraces innovation and collaboration, leading to enhanced outcomes for students, teams, and the entire organization.

Educational coaching involves more than just imparting knowledge and skills. Counselors are crucial in guiding and supporting educators as they adopt and integrate new tools, pedagogy, and technology into their practice. Counselors assist educators in understanding the "why" behind their actions, addressing fears and anxieties, and fostering a supportive environment for professional learning. By focusing on small wins and celebrating progress, counselors empower educators to build confidence and momentum as they strive for continuous improvement. In schools and beyond, counselors serve as advocates, nurturing connections among various community stakeholders to establish a supportive environment.

While this chapter is about defining an EdTech coach, it also has to tackle all aspects of coaching. One of the most essential parts of coaching is listening and receiving feedback. Coaching also has to consider how we meet all our learners' needs. So, as we define this role, we must also address the areas that ensure we are "doing all the things" that a good coach does.

The Importance of Feedback Loops in Coaching

Have you ever done something in your classroom that an administrator saw you do, but you never heard what they thought? It's odd to put time and effort into something and then not get information or recognition on how a lesson went, what you can improve upon, or just general information on how to move forward. That is where feedback loops come in.

Feedback loops involve continuous feedback from the coach, including praise for progress and constructive suggestions for improving goals. There is a lot to consider in the feedback loop, and it is incredibly rewarding to take the time to see what is working and consider ways to improve.

As a coach, you must check in often with your students and provide clear guidance, explanations, and support based on each individual's needs. We frequently refer to the classroom as "personalized learning," where you and your students reflect on the learning to determine where to go next.

For coaches, feedback loops are one of the best ways to build relationships and trust and foster growth. In education, your feedback looks like a cyclical process that checks for understanding, provides support, and uses the information to adjust training and goals for those you coach. You should also have a feedback loop between you and those you coach that allows them to provide you with insights and information on how the training is going and what they need from you. This can be a highly complex flow chart of arrows that continuously grows and cycles back to you and those you work with.

Let's break down each part of that cycle within feedback loops with a real-life example to help you be a stronger coach and help those you support to succeed in the relationship.

You are a coach and working with a team of first-grade teachers. The teachers are of varied expertise and time in the classroom. Some are new to tech, while others are still new to the school. You were asked to work with this group because they were instructed to add more digital literacy and computer science to their schedules. Most of the group has trepidation about adding more to their plate, while others fear that they just don't know enough about the subject to integrate it into their routines. Within this group, you have some early adopters of technology and some that would do packets and direct instruction instead.

While this scenario is realistic, if it doesn't match what you do, just insert the grade level, subject matter you're working with, and so on, and make it work for you. Implementing a feedback loop will be the same if it's done right, and as a coach, you must maximize the impact on student learning. Remember, coaches are often TOSAs (teachers on special assignments), which are typically the first jobs cut if there is a budget shortage. You need to be able to measure success at all levels, from students to teachers to coaches. You must be flexible and able to work with various abilities, talents, and overall interests.

Listening First

The best thing you can do to get started is to listen to the groups and individuals without offering any help. And we mean really listen. Even if you disagree or have heard their concerns a hundred times, you must listen. It's the best way to start building relationships and show you are open to communication.

Actively listen to their story, concerns, and feelings on the topic. Ask clarifying questions, and make sure you understand what they are saying. Use phrases like "it sounds like" or "if I am hearing you correctly," and paraphrase what they said to confirm your understanding. Watch for nonverbal cues as well, such as folded arms or an appearance of being easily distracted. Are they making eye contact with you and leaning into the conversation? If not, this could mean they are not entirely on board with this discussion. Make sure you acknowledge their feelings and keep yours in check. While you might strongly support the proposed changes, it's best to keep that to yourself and just listen.

Put yourself in the shoes of those you're coaching as you explore how to help them. Ask them to provide examples of times they were successful or felt a lesson didn't go as well as it could have. To start the discussion, recall a time you had a lesson that didn't go well when using technology. For instance, the internet might have gone down, preventing anyone from logging in and causing the activity to flop.

The other big part of listening is to focus on the emotions. Validate those feelings. If someone says they feel unprepared to teach computer science, you can understand that fear. Dig deeper into it, and ask them what they need. It may be professional learning, or they just need help going over the vocabulary. Or, they may benefit from you walking through a lesson they recently did and showing them where they are already infusing computer science or where a lesson could easily be tweaked to include these new objectives.

In the end, make sure both of you feel that your goals align before you move on from the listening stage of a feedback loop.

Observations and Modeling Lessons

Once you have listened and set achievable goals, observe the teacher, flip it, and let them observe you doing a lesson with elements you both determined needed to change. Bring in some fun robots or do a basic coding activity in the example we previously discussed integrating digital literacy and computer science. Or, you can observe how the teacher runs their class and how they interact with the students. All of those observations will give you ideas on how you can offer feedback for the small shifts you may want them to make.

After the initial observation, discuss what went well in the lesson and where you see room for improvement. This could be a discussion on student engagement, the difficulty of the material, and how well the learning objectives were met. If the teachers are open to it, ask the students how they feel about the lesson. Hearing from students can be difficult for some teachers, so leave this part out if they are uncomfortable initially. You can support a stronger community by encouraging teachers to engage students; allowing them to offer feedback on a lesson can be very eye-opening.

LessonLoop is an excellent company that evaluates student engagement. It explores eight areas of student engagement and has students answer simple questions about a lesson, such as their level of engagement in the content, what parts were most helpful, what was confusing for the student, and how they generally feel. These eight areas are beneficial during your coaching feedback loops as well.

We know that everything comes down to relationships. This is underscored in the coaching cycles and when we discuss feedback loops. A person must feel valued and like they belong, so tailoring your experiences and interventions based on these discussions will help you stay on task within your coaching cycle. Codesigning the learning by listening and offering varying ways to meet the goals can drive success and strengthen the relationships.

 **Aimee**

Moments ... life is a series of moments. When you are going through a tough time, remember that it's just a fleeting moment that will eventually pass. When the moments are good, embrace them, for they only last so long. Always try to be in the present moment. This philosophy has guided me through difficult times and the best of times.

So, when given a moment to understand your group of learners, please do so. I started this practice early in my career. Because I was a "special subject teacher," I often saw over 300 students within a year. It's a lot to remember—especially as someone who cannot remember names; that is definitely not my strength.

Early in my career, I decided to keep track of not only my students' names, attendance, and grades but also their strengths, weaknesses, and other aspects of their personalities that helped me get to know them as learners and humans. As a technical person, I kept a clipboard with student lists attached to it that had ample room for me to write notes next to each student's name. I did this for years. If a student quickly caught on to a skill I was teaching them, if their favorite color was blue, if they mentioned to me that they disliked something, or if I noticed them requesting to use the bathroom a lot—I wrote it all down.

What did I do with that information? I was able to manage my classroom in a way like never before. I provided students who were "restless" the opportunity to stand at their computers while instruction took place instead of forcing them to sit. I understood who learned by doing and afforded them the challenge of being independent learners by providing tutorials they could follow as I worked with students who needed me to demonstrate a skill before they could accomplish it on their own.

I allowed my students to get out of their seats and assist one another, as long as their hands were behind their backs and they didn't touch the mouse and do the task for the individual they were helping, thus teaching them how to give verbal directives. I understood which students could work together in groups and which students had personality conflicts, and I would assign them accordingly; we need to teach how to handle adversity, you know.

I used this same practice when I coached adults. I took notes on the little things, the big things, the moments. Taking little notes on the individuals you work with helps, especially when your life can become chaotic. Try it: Take a moment and jot down a few notes; this will make you more personable.

How do you determine all the stakeholders and elements on which you want to gather information? Decide how specific you need to be and your ultimate goal within that feedback loop. Remember that the ultimate goal is that your self-reflections and participant reflections should foster opportunities to transform your practice and learn something new.

The first part of any feedback loop is building a community; it should be more than sharing names and titles. If it's a group setting, do activities that engage your audience and allow them to get to know each other. This is an excellent opportunity to begin relationships that will continue to grow throughout the coaching and training cycles. As mentioned before, engagement is incredibly important. We also talked about listening more than offering solutions. All parties must be heard and understood as you are building those relationships.

There are a few other factors to consider when using feedback loops. Sometimes, the answers are going to be uncomfortable. Sometimes, they might feel like a personal affront. You must be open to changing your approach to help others embrace change. There might also be some things you cannot change. Expect roadblocks, but stay positive that you can solve these problems. But if you cannot, accept that and move on. You may need to end the coaching cycle before all parties deem it done for various reasons, and you must also accept that. You may often feel there is more that you could have or would have done for various reasons but know you did what you could with the time you had.

The final part to consider is confidentiality. If you want relationships to be strong, you need to keep those conversations between the parties that matter and leave out the rest. Without trust, there cannot be forward movement.

A good feedback loop will have interaction between all parties for a specific purpose. It could be using a new reading curriculum, adding more inquiry, or creating a project-based learning environment. Whatever goals the parties agree on must go through many iterations before the goal can be achieved. The information gathered, the goals outlined, and the actions taken should benefit and promote a transformative change. Consider what is missing from your feedback cycle if this isn't the case. Your goals and actions should benefit all parties involved, but in the end, you know you are coaching others to help the students. Students are why we do what we do and must be considered at all parts of the loop.

Let's look at an example.

Your district just purchased a virtual reality (VR) kit. (VR is an emerging technology that immerses the viewer in either a 360 image or video. Many VR companies offer interactive experiences that let users fly drones, change the oil in a car, or weld in a virtual space.) You have been tasked with getting teachers trained to use VR in the classroom in various ways. Typically, you would hold some PD, create a sign-out sheet, possibly spend time in classrooms to model it, and then expect the VR kit to be used throughout the school year.

Over time, that VR kit might collect dust or end up in one teacher's classroom, where it's used relatively often. However, considering a coaching model with a feedback loop, you would follow up with all parties to see how the learning has progressed. You would be using surveys, observations, and discussions to see what is working and what more needs to be done to ensure that the VR kit is being used to increase student engagement and learning or whatever goals you set. This loop might include other stakeholders, like the community and administration, to see how the kit is utilized. In this loop, all parties are invested and active in the rollout of this new technology.

Using feedback loops can allow more innovation and more positive experiences to happen. If leveraged correctly, feedback loops can create transformative interactions in the classroom. Just like all of the students in your classroom have different needs and experiences, you will find that when you coach, you will always have to adjust your training to meet the needs of each individual teacher. Your quality feedback loops can help identify the needs of those you coach, help you find strategies and solutions to implement and foster a valuable outcome.

 **Laurie**

Over the past 10+ years of coaching, I have explored numerous EdTech products. Each one offers solutions and ideas to bring excitement to the classroom. Many of these tools fill a need, save time, or make learning fun. My challenge has always been to tie it to the content, which varies considerably from grade to grade, subject to subject, and even day to day.

There's not a single workshop, training, or webinar that will provide exactly what each teacher needs; I know each participant in my training has a different lens. My lens is EdTech, and I look at the tools I train on as opportunities for student learning. However, I know that each participant has a different focus: one might want their students to be stronger readers, while another might be tackling long division.

Identifying what is needed in a PD session is a challenge. As an early adopter of technology in the classroom, I often looked at the trailblazers who came before me. I had to look outside my school to find people globally who offered courses on topics I was interested in. I learned from them how to use the tech I had available in the classroom.

At first, I focused on the tech alone, but over time, I realized that the tool wasn't the answer, at least not entirely. I had to also look at the correct way to implement the technology. I had to think about the quality of the pedagogical approach I was using and how I measured success through formative and summative assessment. And I also needed to see if the technology filled a real need or if it was just the shiny new thing to try.

With the help of feedback loops, I could look at the tool, the pedagogy, and the needs of those I trained to make informed decisions that could drive improvement. Now, I use feedback loops to gather information from those who attend my training. I analyze the data to find gaps and customize future training opportunities so I can reevaluate and adjust accordingly.

I started with exit surveys, which showed me some of my early flaws. I often gave too much information and spent little time on exploration and discovery. I was the "sage on the stage," as they call it, instead of the "guide on the side." But after many iterations, I now offer more time for independent exploration with my support and time for participants to build something they can use immediately after a PD session.

Using feedback loops allowed me to make informed, data-driven decisions. It allowed for more effective training and implementation from those who attended my workshops. And in the end, students benefited from teachers who left my training and were able to leverage the tools appropriately.

Learner Variability

Whenever you look around your classroom, you know that each student has different needs, preferences, backgrounds, and experiences. This is the same no matter the students who fill your classroom. Regardless of the composition of your classroom, this principle applies universally. Whether coaching one-on-one or in a group, you must consider how you present and how the information is received. You must know how to alter, accommodate, and adjust based on the group's needs.

Although this book's focus is on coaching the adult learner, you may want to explore the resources available to support your students by scanning the QR code. One of the most comprehensive websites offering strategies to support all students is Digital Promise. If you are still becoming familiar with Digital Promise's work, you will be astounded by what it has to offer. Through research, advisory boards, and more, this company looks to shape the future of learning. For you, it is a treasure trove of support, including information, strategies, blogs, webinars, and ideas that will serve you well in any aspect of education.

Digital Promise

One of the most impactful parts of Digital Promise is its Learner Variability Navigator. Here you will find resources and strategies to support all learners' needs. As you explore, you will likely go down the rabbit hole, so bookmark the pages you most need and want to refer to. You can also create workspaces on their site to keep all the strategies together.

Thinking about the strategies we use to facilitate learning, let's consider your own experiences in school. What are your oldest memories? What sticks out to you as a transformative moment, either positive or negative? How did you like to study, do your homework, or interact in class? Your preferences helped you hone your strengths and practice skills needed for the workforce. For most people, school is not a transformative experience. Instead, it's a rigid, rule-following, conforming experience that does not meet all needs.

But suppose you flip that narrative and focus on meeting the needs of each student by personalizing the opportunities. In that case, they will feel nurtured and better positioned to reach their full potential. When that happens, our students have the propensity to find a fulfilling career and meet the needs of the workforce.

Because we come from different backgrounds, experiences, expectations, and so on, we must consider how to address each person's needs. Otherwise, our training of others will fall short, frustrating both sides of the coaching framework. We need to honor our diversity and understand one another's feelings, needs, and fears about changing how we teach.

Digital Promise
Adult Learner Factors

The Digital Promise Learner Variability Navigator

Digital Promise focuses on four primary areas for adult learners. These are the learner's background, social emotional learning, cognition, and adult literacies. We will explain each of these in the coaching context; you can scan the QR code to visit the Digital Promise site and learn more.

Adult literacies encompass cognition, social emotional learning, and the learner's background, so it's an excellent place to start. Here, you will consider the learner's background, how they express and communicate their ideas, their comfort level with technology, and how well they problem-solve. Think about a time you were in a meeting when someone commented about their comfort level with the material, fears, or excitement over something. How "lit" they are in these areas will help you understand where to start and give you some strategies to support learners.

Cognition

Cognition is how we think, process, reason, and remember information. It explores how those you coach might need support. Some will want to do research, some wish to have multiple check-ins, and others might request a video or will only respond to you with audio messages. Understanding their preferences regarding how they want to get and give information will help you meet their needs.

Social Emotional Learning (SEL)

Social emotional learning has gained significant attention, particularly since 2020. This is partially due to the considerable disruptions caused by the pandemic. This heightened awareness stems from recognizing that strong social and emotional skills are crucial for navigating challenges, building resilience, and fostering well-being in an increasingly complex world.

Before 2020, SEL was already gaining traction with a shift in attention to mental health issues. However, the pandemic underscored the importance of these skills in addressing the mental health challenges faced by students, educators, and families alike. The isolation highlighted the need for individuals to develop effective strategies for managing emotions, building relationships, and making responsible decisions.

Hundreds of studies showcase the importance of SEL and its impact on our students. These studies all identify four areas where it can help: mental health, skill development, school culture, and academic achievement. The same can be said for those we coach; how we feel can have positive or adverse effects based on bias, emotions, and cognition. We want those we coach to be excited to see us and, in turn, be open and honest during our interactions.

Learner Background

Learner background has a variety of components. For instance, how much sleep we get, our social support at work and home, our physical well-being, and how safe we feel can all affect how we react and learn at every opportunity.

Digital Promise
Learner Variability
Navigator Resources

You can check out the Digital Promise Learner Variability Navigator resources (scan QR code) if you need strategies and support in these areas.

Now that we have defined the role of a coach, you might be asking yourself, why would anyone want to be a coach? We promise it will be gratifying and offer you many opportunities to grow and support others. In the next section, we will explore the "why" of coaching.

Chapter 3

From Draft to Reality
~ The Power of Educational Coaching ~

"When we know WHY we do what we do, everything falls into place. When we don't, we have to push things into place."

—**Simon Sinek** (author and inspirational speaker)

But, why? Why did you want to become a coach?

Children are well-known for their inquisitiveness. They often ask numerous questions, particularly the ubiquitous "why." This natural curiosity drives them to seek understanding before accepting information as fact. If one were to ask a child why they ask "why," it is likely they would respond, "because I want to know."

Similarly, you should also be curious about your profession and practice. At some point, you may be asked about your approach and strategy—whether by a veteran teacher you've been coaching for a while or during a job interview. Even if you're not asked, understanding your "why" can help you stand out and enhance your candidacy.

Establishing Your Why
Resource

Discovering your "why" can make your work more meaningful and fulfilling. Take a moment to read our stories and define your "why" by scanning the QR code and using it as a resource to help you get started.

Why We Became Coaches

Coaching might seem overwhelming at first with its many aspects—there is just so much to think about. We are only in chapter two, and we have already given you so much to consider based on your role, how everyone you support is different, and that we always need to improve. This is a lot to think about for someone coming out of the classroom and into coaching. Now is a good time to share how we got into the coaching arena.

Laurie's Story

As a sixth-grade teacher, I had the opportunity to pilot a 1:1 iPad rollout in 2013. The seven educators on my team were handed the iPads two weeks before school started and told to try them out and see what we thought. I was so excited to try out this new technology. I had never used an iPad before, so I had much to learn. With my students, we made movies, tried different apps, and created images and presentations on this new technology.

I saw a massive increase in engagement and found ways to make learning fun with technology. But for me, the biggest gain was that I suddenly could hear from all my students. I used a program called Nearpod that allowed every student to answer questions, draw things, and interact simultaneously and in the moment. It was a game-changer for me.

I quickly learned all I could about this technology. I paid out of my own pocket for webinars and programs to get me up to speed on using this technology in the classroom. I joined social media to follow others and see how they used the technology we now had access to. I listened to my students to see what they found helpful and looked for ways to enrich my lessons using the iPads.

It was a complete energy shift for me. This is what school should feel like, and it mimicked more of what the "real world" was like when I worked for an insurance company before entering education. Finally, I felt like schools could meet the needs of the current and future workforce if we spent time teaching students and teachers how to harness emerging technologies, innovate, and create opportunities by using technology effectively.

Once I felt confident in my skills and had a few years of experience, I approached the administration about moving into a coaching role. Since it was new, I could design the position to meet the goals of the district and the ones I had learned through experience, research, and coursework. I fell in love with EdTtech and coaching and knew this would be where I spent the rest of my working career.

Aimee's Story

My "why" is a collection of my personal and professional educational experiences.

Having taught "special" subject areas, such as the arts or computer technology, where I could reach every single student in the school, I noticed how I was making small ripples in the body of water we call education. Aside from introducing students to various technical skills, I also noticed that my teaching style differed vastly from my peers. After a while, I didn't even view myself as a "teacher" in the classroom. I saw myself more as a project manager who ensured my learners understood the requirements of their role within my classroom and then the content that was being presented.

I believed in peer and self-evaluation before teacher evaluation. I believed in authentic experiences teaching soft and technical skills first. My rubrics were set up to allow my learners to advocate for their learning while pushing them to reach their highest potential—not just earning an "A."

As mentioned earlier, I simultaneously became the official "unofficial" educational technology coach when I entered my teaching career. I assisted teachers in my building and beyond in implementing technology and showed them small ways to change their instructional practices.

My decision to leave the classroom did not happen overnight. I became a teacher because, well, number one (and most importantly) of that feeling, that "high" you get when you transform your knowledge into others' learning. You have to admit, it's pretty damn magical. Reason number two stems from my disgust with the educational system and hope to make a change, having gone through the system myself and my collective experiences on how school failed me as a learner.

When I became a mother and had children, I reflected on my career goals. It was as if they were the final piece of the educational puzzle that I needed. Up to this point, I have been a teacher, a coach, and an administrator. But man, as a parent, my momma bear claws came out. I now had children going through the educational system, and I was like, come on—we can do better. My children, "our children," deserve better than this.

I am by no means a mathematician. But at this point in my career, I sat back and looked at the "big picture" and reflected upon the small ripples I'd made in the pond I called a classroom. I had this courageous thought that I could multiply my ripples and cause a wave when reaching out to adult learners who, in return, would touch the lives of many children.

I know I am only a small pebble, making a tiny ripple in a large body of water that's inundated with propaganda, state testing, failed initiatives, politics, and poor leadership. I can go on, and most likely, so can you. I wanted to make a difference, hoping it would catch a more significant wave, even if only one ripple at a time.

Why Coaching Is Important for Student Achievement

If we want educators to integrate technology into their teaching practices effectively, we need to offer training and support. Coaching will help educators integrate technology effectively to increase student engagement, personalize the learning experience, and enhance learning outcomes.

We know that motivation is often a frustrating element of teaching. Getting students to be motivated to learn is a question that frequently comes up in professional learning, faculty meetings, and one-on-one coaching exchanges. However, technology offers ways to make learning more interactive. Teachers can

The Challenge with
Gen Z
Simon Sinek

implement tech tools to create a more dynamic and captivating lesson to hold students' attention.

We also know that the younger generations (Gen Z and Gen Alpha) are used to learning differently and often struggle with communication. Let's teach students how to deal with difficult tasks through communication and personalized learning experiences. We can find ways to customize support that will, in turn, enhance learning outcomes. Scan the QR code to listen as Simon Sinek discusses the challenges with Gen Z and shares the very blunt truths behind leadership in today's world.

As coaches, we can help enhance learning outcomes by aligning technology integration with curriculum goals, formative assessments, data tracking, quality feedback, and reflection. We must support our teachers in these incredible challenges so they are equipped instead of overwhelmed. As a coach, you can support technology needs, troubleshoot, listen, and guide teachers through all the challenges they may face in the classroom. Without support, teachers will feel overwhelmed and burned out. Technology can help solve some of these issues but also cause strong feelings.

To help us understand the impact of technology on coaching, we will explore how emerging technology relates to effective coaching. We will break this down based on the technology trends of the 2024–2025 school year, but you can insert whatever new technology you face.

An EdTech coach can often be teachers' first exposure to navigating and integrating new technology into their teaching practice. We aim to empower our educators with the knowledge and skills necessary to harness the power of technology to lead to transformative learning experiences for their students.

Integrating tech, though, can add to teachers' anxiety, as they already have so much on their plate. If you can help those you coach implement these emerging technologies effectively, it can transform learning and support their growth.

Using Virtual Reality (VR)

VR can create immersive learning experiences and allow visualization of how technology can look in the classroom. It's more than just a virtual field trip; it's about the engagement that can happen when students explore in VR. We know that VR can allow learners to visit historical landmarks, practice skills, and even create within the VR world. However, they can also learn about ecosystems, visit places they may never see, and learn essential skills like changing the oil in their car or visiting an assembly line to learn how things are made. VR opens doors, gives access, and can personalize the learning.

Training our teachers to look beyond the thrill of immersive environments to use them to create immersive learning experiences is something we, as tech coaches, can foster. You can also leverage this for coaching opportunities by instilling fun "brain breaks" or brainstorming sessions on how this technology can help with social-emotional needs or even regulation strategies.

Artificial Intelligence (AI)

AI has been buzzing since the release of ChatGPT in November of 2022. But AI has been around for over 70 years. You already use AI when you write an email, select a video to watch on Netflix, or use GPS in your car. AI can be a personal tutor or a sidekick, and it can provide support for anything your teachers and their students need or want to know about the world. It can save teachers time in the building of resources and activities for the classroom. AI can also assist teachers in grading via an AI-made rubric and help teachers look for strategies to support student success. Because of the amount of data that AI pulls from, it can offer data-driven results.

Despite AI's benefits, it's also important to be wary of this technology. Large language models like ChatGPT are inherently flawed and still in their infancy. We are only at the tip of the iceberg here, and so much more will change as AI gets better. EdTech coaches can now use AI to help identify areas where technology can most impact individual students. It can offer learning analytics trends and ideas for implementing any SMART goal.

Aimee and Laurie's Curated Favorite Books and AI Tools

Remember bias, accessibility, and ethical implications, and be aware that hallucinations are possible. There are some fantastic books on the market about how and why to use AI in the classroom and ones that will help you consider both the positive and the negative sides.

Scan this QR code to look at Aimee and Laurie's curated favorite books and AI tools.

Adaptive Learning Platforms

With the technological advances we are undergoing, a revolution is happening for our students with special needs. Tools that translate and read text from images and PDFs, offer audio and visual support, and can 3D print anything we need are available. AI can also make adaptive learning possible through its ability to adapt content and instruction.

Game-Based Learning

Don't forget to bring play to your training sessions and spend time in the classroom. Use any AI tool, such as those listed on Wakelet, to help you create short and innovative games with anything you have available—go ahead and try it.

Create your prompt, or if you need some help, here's one to get you started:

Create a team-building game about grizzly bears and hibernation using only LEGO bricks, pencils, and index cards. This game should not have a winner but teach students facts about bears and hibernation while fostering their SEL skills. We used Gemini to create the game. Scan the QR code to see what it generated.

LEGO Bear Den Game
Created with Gemini

As an EdTech coach, your role will always evolve. You must deeply understand educational technology, pedagogy, and a growth mindset. By embracing these different roles, you can guide educators in integrating technology effectively. Emerging technologies, while exciting, need to be integrated to create immersive and personalized learning experiences that utilize effective pedagogy.

You need to have a deep understanding of UDL (Universal Design for Learning, which is explored in depth in chapter four) and design thinking so that you can provide valuable guidance around creating inclusive and effective learning environments. As your role evolves, you must continue navigating the complexities of an educational landscape. Our dedication to supporting students and empowering teachers drives our mission.

While technology is always changing, your role as a coach will also change. Your role has never been more vital, and with budget constraints and a lack of people entering the education field, you may have to advocate for this position. Let's explore how you can define and propose an EdTech coaching role. You can look for growth or further development areas if you are already in that position.

The EdTech Coach:
A Cornerstone of Educational Innovation

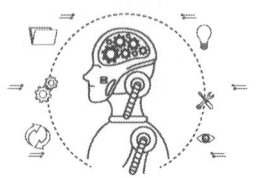

Let's consider the impact of having an educational technology coach in your district or school building and emphasize the importance of advocating for this crucial role. It's 2025, and technology has largely taken over every aspect of our lives, from banking to shopping, checking in for doctor visits, and getting our news. It's almost impossible to go a day without using it.

The U.S. Department of Education: National Educational Technology Plan

Despite this digital revolution, school districts still need to work on embracing technology to enhance learning. To assist us nationally, the U.S. Department of Education released the "2024 National Educational Technology Plan (NETP): A Call to Action for Closing the Digital Access, Design, and Use Divides" in January 2024 to help leverage the educational technology landscape. With this national effort and understanding the importance of bridging the gap in technology and its practical uses in education, an educational technology coach is an essential component to success (scan the QR code learn more). Without one, it's like having a football team without a coach—chaos! Educators need technology coaches to help them integrate technology into the classroom and take learning to the next level. It's why you are reading this book.

If your school or district lacks an educational technology coach, advocating for creating one will involve presenting a compelling case highlighting the benefits for students, teachers, and overall academic outcomes. Advocating for an educational technology coach is a thrilling opportunity to shape the future of education in your school or district. By gathering compelling evidence of the benefits of technology integration and forming a robust professional learning network, you can champion the cause for a more technologically advanced and effective learning environment.

As you develop your proposal for a position, envision how an educational technology coach will elevate your school's academic goals. Craft a detailed job description tailored to your school's needs, and embark on an exciting journey toward a more tech-savvy and engaging educational landscape! This is also an exciting way to utilize free generative AI tools such as Gemini, Microsoft CoPilot, or ChatGPT to help you craft your description.

It's important to remember that while job descriptions are typically written by human resource personnel, department administration, school boards, etc., it may be beneficial for you to contribute your thoughts or suggestions, especially if you are advocating for a position that has not yet been established in your school or district. Even if an educational technology coaching position is already available at your school/district and you are fulfilling that role, understanding the typical attributes of an EdTech coach (ETC) job description could be helpful.

Please take a moment to scan this QR code to review the job summary for a K–12 position.

Sample Job Summary for a K12 Position

Ensure that your proposal also outlines an implementation plan and includes a timeline for rolling out the position. Make certain to emphasize how integrating technology can personalize learning, increase student engagement, and improve academic outcomes. Also, highlight how an educational technology coach can provide ongoing professional development, help teachers effectively integrate technology, and alleviate tech-related challenges they face.

Additionally, illustrate the long-term cost benefits, such as improved teacher efficiency, better use of existing technology investments, and potential grant opportunities. If available, share results from teacher or student surveys indicating a need or desire for more support with technology integration.

It's also a good idea to prepare a cost analysis and suggest potential funding sources, such as reallocating existing resources, applying for grants, or partnering with educational technology companies. Consider partnering with your business administrator or another administrator who would like to embrace an ETC in their building for help.

Finally, put all this information together in a document and develop a clear and concise presentation tailored to your audience, whether it's a principal, superintendent, or school board. Make a presentation for each audience; visual aids like slides, graphs, and charts can effectively illustrate your points. AND, be sure to practice your presentation to ensure clarity and confidence. After all, practice makes perfect!

Chapter 4

Coaching Thoughtfully
~ An Integrated Project Delivery ~

"Good buildings come from good people, and all problems are solved by good design."

—Stephen Gardiner (architect, teacher, and writer)

In previous chapters, we've established the foundation for effective coaching by focusing on relationship building and feedback. It's time to delve deeper into the theoretical frameworks and models underpinning our practice. This chapter will explore key educational models, such as UDL and international technology standards, and demonstrate how they can be applied to create more impactful coaching experiences. By understanding these concepts, we can better tailor our approach to individual learners, foster a supportive learning environment, and maximize the potential for growth and development.

Understanding various educational frameworks is crucial for effective planning and meeting learners where they are, whether coaching children or adults. Good teaching becomes good coaching. As a teacher, you recognize the importance of understanding your student's learning preferences and providing them with the necessary support. This gives you what it takes to transition from an effective teacher into the role of a great coach. It's essential to note that many of the strategies and structures that you implemented to support your students' learning are also applicable when working with adults.

Universal Design for Learning

The UDL Guidelines by CAST

Universal Design for Learning (UDL) is a proactive framework for creating flexible learning environments accommodating diverse learner needs. The organization CAST (Center for Applied Special Technology) describes UDL as "a framework to improve and optimize teaching and learning for all people based on scientific insights into how humans learn." Please scan the QR code to learn more about CAST and its latest version of UDL principles.

Did you read that? It said "humans." Not strictly children—humans.

Before we continue, please take a moment to scan the QR code and watch the video titled "Why We Need UDL."

Why We Need Universal Design Michael Nesmith TEDxBoulder

Let's pause for a moment and consider this: Children who face learning challenges or have unique learning preferences often carry those characteristics into adulthood. It's essential to keep this in mind when working with adults. Whether you are setting up an in-person professional development session or a digital step-by-step tutorial, the principles of UDL will help you develop and create the best environment for your learners. This also implies that when coaching educators in their classrooms, it's important to be cognizant of various learners' needs when implementing technology. The UDL framework is based on neuroscience research and educational psychology, emphasizing multiple means of representation, engagement, and expression.

Frameworks such as the Universal Design for Learning (UDL) will help guide and support your efforts to provide flexible learning environments that accommodate diverse learner needs. As a coach, you can help teachers integrate interactive and collaborative tools and provide training on digital content-creation tools and accessibility features for diverse learners. But first, let's explore learner variability a bit more.

The three facets of UDL explained:

Multiple Means of Engagement: The "Why" of Learning

The principle of Multiple Means of Engagement is a crucial aspect of effective learning design, focusing on designing learning experiences that are meaningful, relevant, and motivating for learners. It emphasizes the need to offer various options and choices to engage with the activities to cater to individual learners' diverse needs and preferences. This can be achieved by incorporating multiple strategies and techniques, such as multimedia presentations, interactive activities, simulations, discussions, and hands-on projects.

Providing learners with multiple means of engagement allows them to learn and demonstrate their understanding in ways that resonate with them, increasing their motivation, engagement, and overall achievement. Ultimately, this approach ensures learners can learn and grow meaningfully and relevantly, which leads to a more positive and fulfilling learning experience.

How can you model Multiple Means of Engagement?

As a coach, you can provide opportunities for the administrators and teachers you coach by creating interactive material. You might utilize a Learning Management System (LMS) like Google Classroom, Canvas, or Schoology so teachers can collaborate with digital and interactive presentations (also an excellent way to collect formative data to help support your endeavor). You can create personalized learning pathways if you're training in a large group (such as by creating digital choice boards or digital educational playlists) to meet each educator's needs.

How can you coach others to implement Multiple Means of Engagement?

Support this principle by helping the teachers you work with integrate interactive and collaborative tools into their lessons. You can coach your teachers using platforms for virtual discussions (such as an LMS), adding gamification elements and personalized learning pathways to increase student engagement.

Multiple Means of Representation: the "What" of Learning

The principle of Multiple Means of Representation focuses on how information is consumed and presented to ensure that it accommodates a variety of learning preferences. This involves providing content in multiple formats, such as text, audio, video, graphics, and hands-on activities. Remember, this is focused on the consumption of information and how your learner wishes to learn.

Allow us to explain it this way:

Say you are creating a tutorial on how to use Kami. In education, Kami enables interactive learning through PDF annotation and collaboration and is an excellent tool to help support the principles of UDL. In your tutorial, you provide text with an example of how to use a screen reader, animated GIFs that accompany your text directions, and various videos that explain what the text says visually. In this scenario, you offer multiple ways for learners to choose their consumption. They can choose to read and look at the animated GIFs. They can listen to your tutorial with a screen reader and review the animated GIFs. Or they can simply watch the embedded videos with closed captioning. The learners have a choice for how they want to consume the information.

Let's consider an example where a tutorial on Kami is almost there but not quite yet. The tutorial initially provides a chunk of text to read describing the first few steps on how to get started and then switches to a video for the "more complicated" parts of Kami. In this scenario, all learners follow the same sequence, which starts with text and moves on to the video. While there is variety in the content delivery, learners don't have a choice in how they want to consume the information; inclusivity is limited since all learners are required to read and watch a video.

Next, we discuss how to implement Multiple Means of Representation in coaching and ensure its integration into practice.

How can you model Multiple Means of Representation?

You can effectively incorporate multiple ways of presenting information in your coaching role. For example, you could create diverse materials for educators to present information in different formats. If you're making an educational technology newsletter for your school's staff, you could include a monthly tips and tricks section introducing technology tools for your district. This digital, interactive newsletter section could include a screencast with closed captions for accessibility.

Consider providing a step-by-step tutorial with text and images for those who prefer written instructions to accompany your video. Applying UDL principles, you can create the content and visuals first and then use them as a guide for creating a video. This way, your newsletter viewers will have a choice in how they want to interact with the content in your tips and tricks section.

How can you coach others to implement Multiple Means of Representation?

To assist teachers in applying this principle, you can encourage them to use multimedia tools and resources in their lessons and coach them on the variety of digital tools that offer accessibility features. Many awesome tools are available to help your teacher friends implement UDL practices. Screencastify, Kami, Microsoft, and Nearpod all have exceptional options to assist you in creating materials that enhance Multiple Means of Representation.

Multiple Means of Action & Expression: The "How" of Learning

The Multiple Means of Action & Expression principle emphasizes providing learners with various options to showcase their knowledge and skills. Why not allow them to demonstrate their knowledge and understanding of a topic by showing you what they know using a medium that they are most comfortable with? Multiple Means of Action & Expression can be accomplished by allowing learners to express themselves through different means, such as writing, speaking, creating multimedia projects, or using assistive technologies.

How can you model Multiple Means of Action & Expression?

We understand that time is of the essence and that often, when coaching and providing professional development opportunities, this principle may go untouched—leaving little room for your learners to demonstrate their understanding and expertise in learning instructional technology. To better support diverse learning preferences, you can offer flexible assessment options to check for understanding at the end of your workshop or meeting. Teachers and administrators could express their learning through a traditional written reflection or a more creative format, such as a video presentation or a blog post.

What does this mean for you as a coach?

You can help teachers implement this principle by introducing them to digital content-creation tools, such as video editing software, digital storytelling platforms, and online presentation tools. Additionally, you can provide training on accessibility features and accommodations for students with diverse learning needs.

Aimee's Story

Throughout the pandemic, online education was challenging. The situation forced us to utilize technology in education in ways we weren't prepared for. At the pandemic's start, I worked for BOCES (Board of Cooperative Education Services) in New York State. While I had prior experience creating and delivering online learning modules for adults and assisting in online educational technology classes at college, the pandemic compelled me to concentrate on providing a fair online learning experience for all learners.

Like many others, the pandemic caused me to rethink my purpose. Due to my learning preferences and abilities, I have always naturally incorporated elements of UDL (Universal Design for Learning), even before I truly understood what they were. Most of the time, administration and teachers requested that I create tutorials personally, as I was told they preferred my explanation over the vendors'. It was flattering.

Throughout my teaching career, I have been a strong advocate for providing choices in my approach to education. Fueled by a newfound passion for micro-credentials and authentic adult learning, I have transformed my online courses into dynamic spaces where educators can connect, collaborate, and revel in their accomplishments. I aimed to cultivate an online community that mirrors the supportive environment I yearned for during my college experience.

I designed a course called "Choose Your Tech Adventure" that allowed learners to select a theme of educational practice and then choose the technology they wanted to master within that theme. The course also incorporated Universal Design for Learning (UDL) principles.

Some of the overarching themes offered in the course were:

- Digital Citizenship and Safety
- Gamification
- Personalized Learning
- Assessments

Within each theme, learners were presented with two choices. For example, under the theme of Gamification, learners could learn the theory and application of gamification and how it could benefit their classroom. They could then follow tutorials for tools like Classcraft or Gamestar Mechanic (both retired products) to learn how to incorporate them into their classrooms.

The tutorials offered various options, including text, animated GIFs, videos, and samples. Additionally, learners had access to virtual office hours and on-demand support for additional help.

Understanding that your audience will come to the table with various learning differences is key to creating and developing in-person and online training materials. It is vital to offer multiple ways for your participants to obtain information and allow them to exemplify what they have learned in multimodal ways.

As mentioned above, the UDL framework provides an inclusive approach to presenting, interacting with, and demonstrating learning. The design thinking process is another effective method for giving educators and students more inclusive and compelling learning experiences. It concentrates on understanding learner needs and developing solutions to address those needs.

What is Universal Design for Learning? Digital Promise

If you need more information about UDL, check out Digital Promise's UDL resources by scanning this QR code.

Technology Aligned Standards

Understanding the principles of Universal Design for Learning (UDL) can help you grow as a coach, reconsider how you convey information, and introduce new technologies to others. Professional learning standards and educational technology frameworks are valuable reference points for educational technology coaches, providing a structure for their work and ensuring that they provide high-quality support to educators using a shared language.

Educational Standards in Technology Education

So, you're in education, huh? You must love acronyms, right? Well, get ready—this section is full of them! Where should we start? We know! Let's start with the ISTE Standards.

The ISTE (International Society for Technology in Education) Standards provide a comprehensive framework that outlines the knowledge and skills students, educators, coaches, and administrators should possess to utilize technology in education effectively. These standards encourage meaningful technology integration across different educational environments, emphasizing educational practices and approaches rather than specific tools.

Why is it important to have an understanding of the ISTE Standards? So glad you asked! The ISTE Standards guide educators, leaders, and coaches on effectively integrating technology into their teaching practices. These standards provide valuable insights for incorporating technology into education and ensure that the implementation is consistent and high-quality. In other words, it provides a baseline. Understanding and integrating these standards into professional development initiatives is essential for educators to stay updated and proficient in leveraging technology for educational purposes. Furthermore, the standards highlight technology's ethical and responsible use, promoting a safe and secure online environment for educators and students. Equally as important, the ISTE Standards also encourage collaboration and networking among educators, fostering a community of learning and innovation in education.

In this book, we will narrow our focus on the ISTE Standards for coaching. For more information on the ISTE Standards, please visit www.iste.org.

ISTE Standards for Coaches

As a coach, your primary goal is to empower educators to enhance their teaching practices. The ISTE Standards for Coaches (scan the QR code to learn more) provide a comprehensive framework to guide you in achieving this objective. These standards are specifically designed to equip instructional technology coaches with the knowledge, skills, and dispositions necessary to support educators in effectively integrating technology into their classrooms.

ISTE Standards for Coaches

Please take a moment to review the seven key areas around which the standards are structured. Each standard is supported by indicators that contribute to the overall standard for coaching. The standards are as follows:

 Change Agent

The ISTE Coaching Standard "Change Agent" emphasizes the vital role of a coach as a catalyst for change. It motivates and empowers educators and leaders to seamlessly integrate technology through a shared vision and provide all learners with fair and equitable access to top-notch education.

Connected Learner

The Connected Learner Standard is all about coaches staying ahead of the curve with the latest educational technologies and practices. These coaches are always learning, expanding their expertise, and teaming up with fellow educators to share knowledge and grow together. They continuously improve their coaching and teaching skills by keeping up with research, seeking feedback, and reflecting on their methods. This standard highlights the value of lifelong learning and the need to stay tuned to the ever-changing world of education.

Collaborator

The Collaborator Standard highlights educators' crucial role in enhancing teaching and learning. Coaches join forces to create and execute engaging, technology-driven learning opportunities, drawing on various viewpoints and skills. They cultivate an environment of collective accountability for boosting student success and encourage the seamless integration of technology in alignment with school objectives. This standard emphasizes the critical role of teamwork in advancing educational outcomes. Remember, sharing is caring. ♥

Learning Designer

The ISTE Coaching Standard for Learning Designer empowers educators to create innovative, inclusive learning experiences integrating technology seamlessly. Coaches guide educators in selecting and leveraging digital tools that promote creativity, critical thinking, and collaboration. By applying Universal Design for Learning (UDL) principles, coaches support educators in designing personalized and accessible learning environments. Through data-driven insights and continuous feedback, coaches help educators refine their learning designs to meet the diverse needs of all students. This standard champions a student-centered learning approach, where technology is a powerful tool for enhancing educational outcomes.

Professional Learning Facilitator

The Professional Learning Facilitator Standard focuses on creating personalized, relevant, goal-aligned professional development. Coaches aim to cultivate active learning environments, encourage collaboration, and integrate research-based best practices for effective technology use. They support educators' growth by promoting reflection and providing ongoing feedback to ensure that professional development (PD) improves teaching and student outcomes. Continuous evaluation is used to refine and sustain PD efforts.

Data-Driven Decision-Maker

The ISTE Coaching Standard for Data-Driven Decision-Maker empowers coaches to guide educators in leveraging data to inform and improve instructional practices. Coaches help educators analyze student performance and engagement data to identify patterns, tailor learning experiences, and address instructional gaps. They prioritize the ethical and responsible use of data, ensuring privacy and confidentiality while using insights to enhance teaching and student outcomes. Through ongoing data analysis and reflection, coaches support educators in refining their strategies for maximum impact.

Digital Citizen Advocate

The ISTE Coaching Standard for Digital Citizen Advocate equips coaches to empower students and educators to become responsible and ethical digital citizens. Coaches address critical issues such as cyberbullying, data privacy, and digital footprints while advocating equitable access to digital resources. Coaches help individuals navigate the digital world confidently and make informed decisions by fostering a culture of respect and critical thinking. Through their guidance, students and educators develop the skills necessary to contribute positively to the online community.

As you advance your coaching career, grounding yourself in the internationally recognized ISTE Standards will provide a solid foundation. Reflect on how each standard and indicator influences all educational community members, from students and teachers to administrators and parents. By aligning your efforts with the ISTE Standards and the specific goals of your academic institution, you can ensure that your work is relevant and impactful and contributes to a thriving learning environment.

Understanding the ISTE Standards for Coaches and the principles of Universal Design for Learning (UDL) equips you with powerful tools to enhance your coaching practice. By nurturing a growth mindset in educators, encouraging collaboration, and strategically integrating technology, you can empower educators to create inclusive and impactful learning experiences for all students. Remember that the journey to becoming an effective coach is a continuous learning process. Embrace these frameworks as a springboard for your professional development, and witness your coaching practice flourish into a powerful force for positive change in the educational landscape.

Chapter 5

Modeling Technology Integration in Coaching
~ Quality Control ~

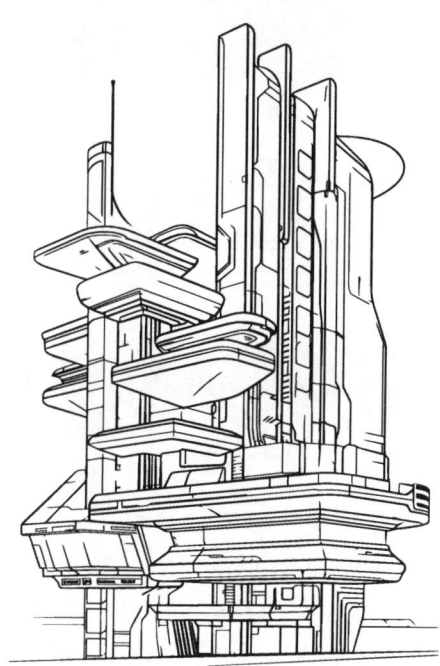

"A great building must begin with the unmeasurable, must go through measurable means when it is being designed and in the end must be unmeasurable."

—**Louis Kahn** (architect)

Educational Technology Frameworks

We've covered setting your own professional goals and understanding the ISTE Standards as a foundation. Now, let's move forward and delve into technology frameworks! An educational technology framework is a structured approach that helps educators and institutions understand, evaluate, and implement technology effectively in learning environments. It provides a blueprint or model for integrating technology into teaching and learning practices.

SAMR

The SAMR (Substitution, Augmentation, Modification, and Redefinition) model is a framework for evaluating the depth of technology integration in the classroom, ranging from simple substitution to transformative redefinition.

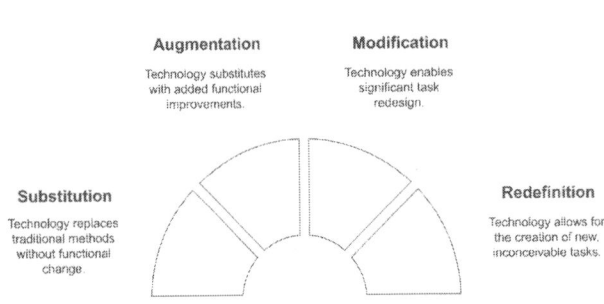

SAMR is the most well-known framework we will explore. Dr. Ruben Puentedura created it to guide the use of technology in the classroom, and each part of the SAMR model represents a different degree of technology integration.

Let's explore each of the four levels using a simple activity you might do in a PD session or while coaching. If you remember when you learned about Bloom's Taxonomy in your teacher preparatory courses, these levels also align with Bloom's.

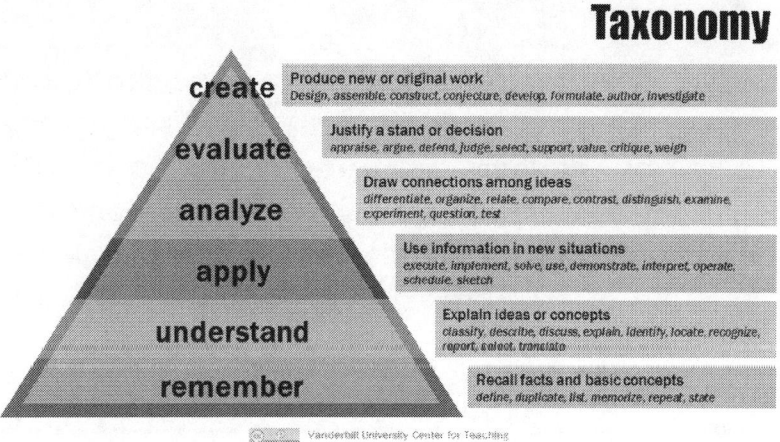

Taxonomy

create — Produce new or original work
Design, assemble, construct, conjecture, develop, formulate, author, investigate

evaluate — Justify a stand or decision
appraise, argue, defend, judge, select, support, value, critique, weigh

analyze — Draw connections among ideas
differentiate, organize, relate, compare, contrast, distinguish, examine, experiment, question, test

apply — Use information in new situations
execute, implement, solve, use, demonstrate, interpret, operate, schedule, sketch

understand — Explain ideas or concepts
classify, describe, discuss, explain, identify, locate, recognize, report, select, translate

remember — Recall facts and basic concepts
define, duplicate, list, memorize, repeat, state

Vanderbilt University Center for Teaching

Substitution

The basic level of SAMR is simply using technology for something you always did on paper. For example, give your participants a handout agenda. But, with substitution, you will have them scan a QR code to gain access or share a web link with them on a Nearpod.

As a technology integrator, you will often see substitution used. Teachers will tell you that they use a lot of technology in their classrooms, but you may observe that they are using it purely as a substitution, such as by having students hand in work on an online LMS instead of putting it in the wire basket at the front of the room. It's not always bad, but it doesn't add much value.

Sometimes, too, it is better to do something offline. The only time substitution can become an issue is if it is the ONLY time you touch technology. If you compare substitution to Bloom's Taxonomy, it aligns with the "remember" level.

Think about your traditional paper worksheet. At the substitution level, you will turn those traditional worksheets into digital ones for students to complete and submit. You will then grade digitally as well.

Augmentation

Simply augmenting your coaching approach can significantly benefit those you support. This may involve demonstrating how to use a program so students can share and discuss their work digitally. Set up a discussion board or a discussion group to facilitate idea sharing related to coaching. Additionally, using chat instead of email for online interactions can enhance communication. While these actions may not seem revolutionary, they represent a more intentional use of technology. This approach corresponds with the "understand" and "apply" levels of Bloom's Taxonomy.

When considering whether the lesson has been augmented, consider whether the same digital worksheet has been substituted. Because of its responsive nature, it may have hyperlinks and interactive elements, offering instant feedback and enhanced engagement.

Modification

Modification could be having your learners take their notes online, keep track of their goals on a shared online site, and then use the data to create a presentation or resource. The modification to the work is that the work itself is often shifted to those you are coaching. Modification can also open doors to more accessibility, where things can be read aloud, font sizes can change based on need, or support documents are linked to online documents. On Bloom's Taxonomy, modification can still be the "apply" level, but it will most likely be the "analyze" level.

At this level, technology has enabled significant redesigning the learning task. Instead of a digital worksheet, a collaborative document may be shared, allowing for real-time collaboration and feedback and keeping a record of any changes. The lesson is more dynamic, encouraging discussions, idea sharing, and peer-to-peer learning.

Redefinition

When we get to this level, we use technology to allow us to do something we could never do without it. It could be creating an online collaborative book, going on a virtual tour, or even creating audio feedback using a tool like Mote to allow for two-way conversations. On Bloom's Taxonomy, this will be the "evaluate" or the "create" levels. Not all technology uses need to be at the "redefinition" level. You can bounce between all four levels of SAMR as you lead activities throughout the day and the school year.

At the redefinition level, the activities will only be possible with technology. You might use technology for virtual visits with experienced researchers, or students can present their learning. The redefinition level is a transformative experience that engages students in real-world experiences where they can create, collaborate, and communicate globally.

TPACK

TPACK stands for Technological Pedagogical and Content Knowledge: Technological Knowledge (TK), Content Knowledge (CK), and Pedagogical Knowledge (PK). TPACK is a model that explores when to use technology through three interlocking areas to find the "sweet spot." You have one circle for your content, one for your teaching methods or pedagogy, and one for technology. Where they meet in the center is the sweet spot for when technology is used effectively to support student learning. It doesn't mean that only having two of the three circles in the lesson is terrible, but it showcases technology as the most effective.

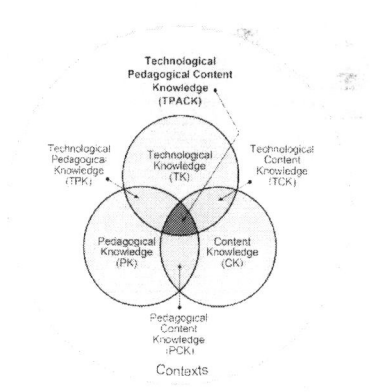

TPACK.ORG

Laurie

Because there was such a considerable time gap between getting my master's in teaching and landing my first teaching job, I had to relearn what good pedagogy was. When I trained on insurance, I found getting the participants to participate was way more fun than me droning on in a traditional lecture style. In my first few years in the classroom, I relied heavily on the teachers around me to reteach the basics. There were certain things they would remind me of often, like "Maslow before Bloom," which is a reminder that students need to have their basic needs met before they can learn.

I also found that when I first used technology in the classroom, I relied heavily on it instead of thinking about how to use it effectively. During my ISTE certification course, I finally dove into TPACK and UDL. It was eye-opening how critical quality pedagogy is for anything in the classroom. We know not everyone in the class learns the same way, so why do we teach them the same way?

We have explored two significant frameworks for using technology in the classroom while exploring how it impacts our coaching. SAMR and TPACK are very subjective but can help you explore, analyze, and adjust your coaching based on the exploration and application of these frameworks. But before we think about using technology, we need to consider the research around Maslow and Bloom a bit.

Maslow's Hierarchy of Needs

This model, built in 1943, proposes that motivation is driven by a series of needs arranged in a pyramid. At the base are our physiological needs, followed by safety, love, belonging, esteem, and final self-actualization. Recognizing and addressing these needs is important in an educational setting before any learning can happen.

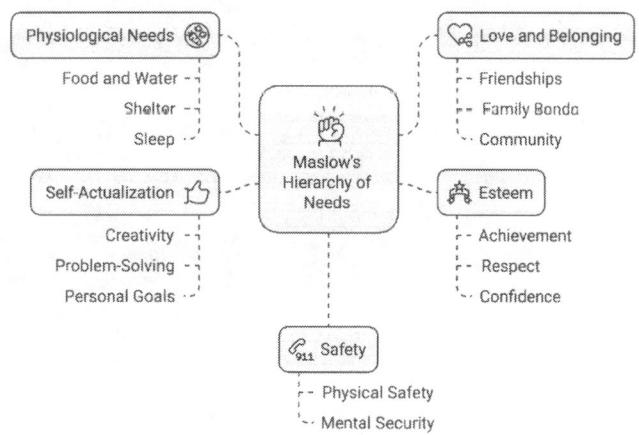

Bloom's Taxonomy

Once these basic needs are addressed, you can implement Bloom's Taxonomy effectively. These cognitive skills range from lower-order thinking (remembering and understanding) to higher-order thinking (analyzing, evaluating, and creating). This progression is more effective when the needs in Maslow's hierarchy are addressed first.

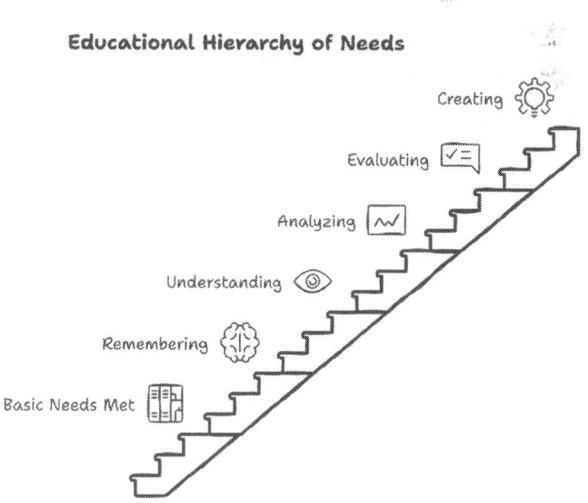

OK, so how does this all relate to TPACK?

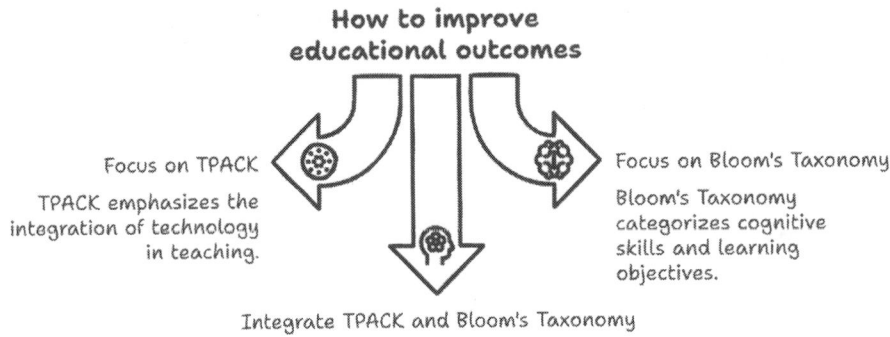

How to improve educational outcomes

Focus on TPACK

TPACK emphasizes the integration of technology in teaching.

Focus on Bloom's Taxonomy

Bloom's Taxonomy categorizes cognitive skills and learning objectives.

Integrate TPACK and Bloom's Taxonomy

Enhance instructional design by combining technology and cognitive skills.

Sounds good, right? You will integrate TPACK levels by integrating technology and cognitive skills to improve educational outcomes. This is an enormous task! But looking at what we can do at each level of Bloom's Taxonomy helps frame how you can implement technology effectively.

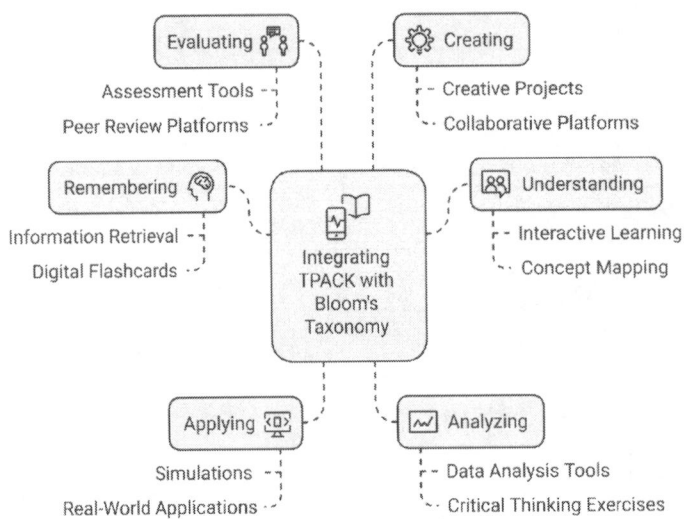

Evaluating
- Assessment Tools
- Peer Review Platforms

Creating
- Creative Projects
- Collaborative Platforms

Remembering
- Information Retrieval
- Digital Flashcards

Integrating TPACK with Bloom's Taxonomy

Understanding
- Interactive Learning
- Concept Mapping

Applying
- Simulations
- Real-World Applications

Analyzing
- Data Analysis Tools
- Critical Thinking Exercises

Triple E

The Triple E framework (authored by Liz Kolb) allows you to run any lesson through a rubric to see how well the technology works. This framework has you answer nine questions about engagement, enhancement, and extension, three areas where technology makes sense. Are students engaged in the learning? Is educational technology adding something to the teaching, and can the understanding extend beyond the lesson and the classroom? If so, you have hit a home run for planning a lesson. This model can work for any group of students, from your youngest to those in your PD sessions.

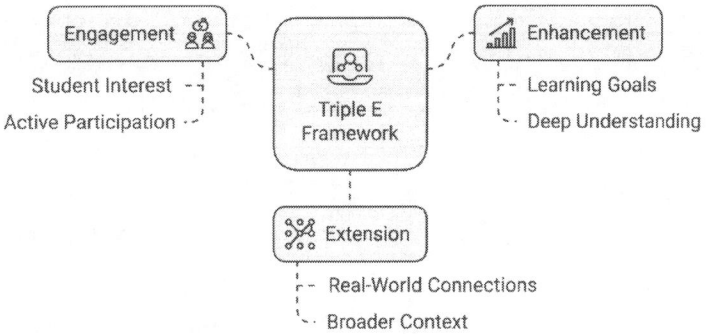

Engagement

At the first level, the framework looks at engagement. This focuses on how the technology can capture students' attention and motivate them to participate actively in their learning. This relates nicely to UDL's Multiple Means of Engagement. Engaging our students means creating an environment where they feel involved and interested in the presented content. This holds true for those in your professional learning workshops as well.

We are often asked, "I'm a math teacher. Will this have something I can use?" Because we want increased participation, collaboration, and enthusiasm for learning, we always answer, "Yes! Everything you learn in this session will support student learning by ..."

Engagement can be obtained using interactive tools, manipulatives, fun activities, and games. Incorporating videos, podcasts, real examples, or real-world connections can help. Remember that you can add in discussions when training or create group projects that will keep the participants in PD engaged and on task.

Enhancement

The second area of this framework is how technology can improve and enrich the learning experience. This means we will not use technology just to say we use technology. Instead, technology will provide deeper insights and experiences. The goal is to create exploration opportunities and engage those critical thinking skills.

Enhancement can involve simulations, like PhET or virtual labs, such as virtual or augmented reality. It can also involve a choice board that allows for personalized learning paths (tie it to teacher content!) and enables the learning to happen individually. This can also be an opportunity to examine the data, analyze performance, and provide targeted feedback.

Extension

The final component of the Triple E framework deals with how learning can extend outside the classroom walls. It encourages us to create opportunities for our participants to apply knowledge in real-world contexts and connect with broader communities. This will help build relevance and create interest.

Bringing in guest speakers or participating in online communities, virtual field trips, and project- or inquiry-based learning experiences that allow for a wider audience than those within your classroom are ways to extend a lesson or PD.

 **Laurie**

There is a small school in upstate New York where the class sizes are at most half a dozen students. The librarian gets her students to interview people through Google Meet to give them a broader worldview. They then do a project related to the field to learn more about careers and the world.

Of course, these frameworks are all subjective, but they help us determine when and where to use educational technology in our classrooms. They give us a starting point for deciding when and where it makes the most sense to add technology to a lesson. If we use any of these frameworks effectively, we will do more for our students by appropriately enriching their learning.

We want to feature our good friend Deann Poleon (follow her on X @DeannPoleon). She is a fantastic technology integrationist who works at a school in the Buffalo area of New York; before tackling technology integration, she was a high school English teacher for many years. What she exceeds at is modeling quality pedagogy with technology integration. She spends her days in various classrooms where her activities are often in the top tiers for SAMR, within the sweet spot of TPACK, and involve all the E's in the Triple E framework.

When teachers ask Deann to visit, they tell her about the content that needs to be covered. Then, Deann uses her magic to create engaging lessons that allow students to learn in ways that transform their learning experience.

For example, when Deann's school wanted to tackle digital citizenship, she helped students create a digital citizenship summit. The summit encouraged students to teach, inspire, and encourage others to be safe and smart online, to be socially responsible, and to use technology for good.

digcitinstitute

But Deann doesn't just do one activity and call it done; she continues to build on the work year after year. She works with the Digital Citizenship Institute (scan the QR code to the left) to bring new experiences to her school every year and also supports global outreach programs like its Global Student Showcases, DigCit Summits, and more.

Scan the QR code, "Make a #DigCitIMPACT with Deann Poleon," to listen to Deann talk about digital citizenship.

Make a #DigCitIMPACT with Deann Poleon

Relationships and student agency are also important to Deann, making her a powerhouse in the technology integration field. For instance, Deann excels in technology integration by collaborating effectively with teachers across all content areas. She understands sound pedagogical principles and can successfully instill student ownership in technology. Deann works with teachers and students of all ages to explore innovative technology applications like robotics and esports. She empowers students to share their knowledge and demonstrate how these technologies can enhance their school experience.

By considering the why, the what, and the how to use technology by leveraging one of these frameworks, you will ensure that technology isn't an afterthought, an add-on, or one more thing. Instead, technology will support quality pedagogy and deepen student understanding. It will help make learning sticky! Think about how you will use these frameworks as you coach others on using educational technology to achieve positive outcomes.

Chapter 6

Educational Coaching Models
~ Constructing a Scale Model ~

"It is not the beauty of a building you should look at; it's the construction of the foundation that will stand the test of time."

—**David Allan Coe** (musician and songwriter)

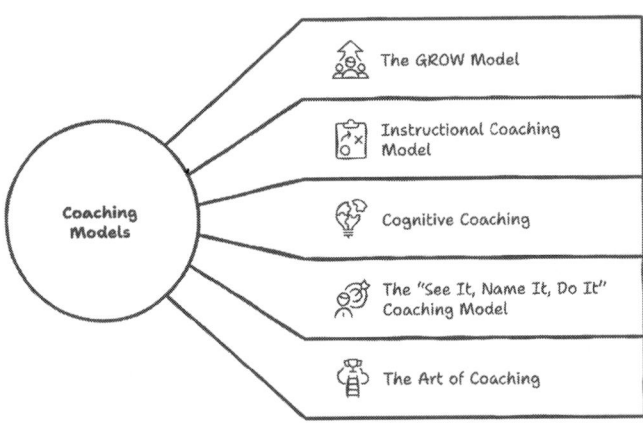

Exploring Diverse Coaching Models in Education

- The GROW Model
- Instructional Coaching Model
- Cognitive Coaching
- The "See It, Name It, Do It" Coaching Model
- The Art of Coaching

In the muck of educational coaching, standards, and frameworks lies a slew of coaching models designed to improve teaching practices, enhance student learning outcomes, and foster professional growth among educators. Determining which one is right for you relies on several factors, including your personality, the culture of your school, current coaching models set in place at your school/district, and so on. Some of the prominent examples of coaching models and frameworks include, but are not limited to:

- The GROW Model
- Instructional Coaching Model
- Cognitive Coaching
- The "See It, Name It, Do It" Coaching Model
- The Art of Coaching

Over the next few pages, we will provide you with a brief overview and resources for exploring more about each example.

The GROW Model

The GROW Model is a simple yet powerful framework for structuring coaching sessions. It focuses on four key components:

The GROW Model
Explained for Coaches

Goal: Define what the coachee wants to achieve.
Reality: Explore the current situation and context.
Options: Identify possible courses of action.
Will: Establish a plan of action and commitment.

Sir John Whitmore and colleagues developed the GROW Model in the late 1980s. It is commonly used in educational settings to help teachers set and achieve professional goals.

Instructional Coaching Model

The Instructional Coaching Model involves coaches working directly with teachers to implement evidence-based instructional strategies. It was popularized by Jim Knight, a prominent figure in the field of education who is known for his extensive work in instructional coaching and professional development. This model emphasizes the partnership philosophy, the use of data, and specific teaching strategies that utilize collaboration, mutual respect, and the importance of evidence-based practices.

The Instructional
Coaching Group
Jim Knight

In this model, coaches navigate through an instructional coaching three-part "Impact Cycle" where coaches like yourself identify, impact, and learn by observing classrooms, providing feedback, modeling instructional techniques, and supporting teachers in applying new strategies.

Cognitive Coaching

Cognitive Coaching
Thinking Collaborative

In the 1980s, Arthur Costa and Robert Garmston developed Cognitive Coaching, a professional development model emphasizing reflective dialogue to promote self-directed learning among educators. Cognitive Coaching aims to empower educators by focusing on their internal thought processes and encouraging them to take ownership of their practices and approaches.

The "See It, Name It, Do It" Coaching Model

The "See It, Name It, Do It" coaching model, developed by Paul Bambrick-Santoyo, is a three-part structured approach to enhancing instructional practices through focused feedback and actionable steps. This model is part of Bambrick-Santoyo's broader efforts in effective school leadership and teacher development.

The "See It, Name It, Do It" coaching model is composed of the following steps:

If You Want Them to
Get It, Get Them to
See It
ascd

See It: This step involves observing and identifying specific instructional practices or behaviors that are successful and those that require improvement. Coaches use guides to help them gather evidence to identify the gaps.

Name It: In this phase, the coach explicitly identifies the key leverage point that will significantly impact student learning. This involves clearly articulating the specific area that needs improvement. The coach should provide concrete examples and explain why this change is a crucial and actionable next step.

Do It: This final step focuses on action with the coach and the teacher collaborating to implement the identified improvement. This could involve role-playing, practicing new strategies, modeling, or developing a step-by-step action plan. The emphasis is on practical application and ensuring the teacher feels confident in making the change.

The Art of Coaching

"The Art of Coaching" by Elena Aguilar presents a holistic and reflective approach to instructional coaching. It emphasizes the development of awareness, the importance of reflection, and the transformation goal. Through building strong, trust-based relationships and focusing on sustainable improvement, this framework aims to empower teachers to enhance their instructional practices and ultimately improve student learning outcomes.

Bright Morning Team

The key components of "The Art of Coaching" are **a**wareness, **r**eflection, and **t**ransformation. Coaches must be aware of the educational environment and encourage self-awareness and teacher awareness. In this reflective practice, questions and journaling are essential for deep reflection. The ultimate goal is to facilitate significant and lasting changes in instructional practices, support mindset shifts, and focus on sustainable improvement.

Vendor-Based Coaching Models and Certifications

In your role, you will often have opportunities to work with various vendors, companies, or individuals who provide educational technology products or services. Vendor coaching programs offer an additional opportunity to enhance your coaching skills.

While some aspects of vendor coaching may be specific to a particular vendor, requiring you to obtain additional certifications such as Google Educator or Apple Teacher, vendors' resources are often proprietary, and the curriculum is based on their research. Additionally, earning badges to showcase your level of achievement can be very rewarding. Among the many coaching certification programs available, we've selected the following offerings from various vendors to showcase:

Google Certified Coach Program

Google Certified
Coach Program

The Google Certified Coach Program is designed to improve educators' skills in integrating technology into their teaching practices. The program is meant to be completed over the school year and consists of four steps, depending on where you are in your Google journey. Step one includes a curriculum focused on developing you as a coach. Step two involves completing the Coach Skills Assessment to demonstrate your knowledge. In step three, you are asked to obtain Level 1 and 2 Google Educator certifications if you have not already completed them.

Finally, the coaching portfolio is designed to reflect many weeks of working one-on-one with teachers. Some key features of the program include a research-based curriculum, opportunities to apply learning in real-world coaching scenarios, and certification.

Apple Learning Coach

The Apple Learning Coach program is a free online certification that teaches coaching skills for integrating technology into learning. Like the Google Certified Coach Program, Apple Learning Coach includes an online certification course and a Coaching Portfolio. Apple Learning Coach uses Everyone Can Create to inspire participants and demonstrate engaging activities for students. It guides educators through a coaching cycle and developing an action plan. Applicants need Apple Teacher recognition and approval from the school, district, or organizational leadership.

Apple Learning Coach

Various coaching models and certifications are available for exploration. A coaching model is a framework or approach that outlines the principles, techniques, and strategies a coach uses. It's a broader concept that can encompass various methodologies and philosophies. A coaching cycle is a structured process that typically involves several stages and is a more specific roadmap within a coaching model, providing a step-by-step approach to guide the coaching relationship. The next section will provide a more detailed description of coaching cycles and what they may look like.

Coaching Cycles

Now that we've explored standards, frameworks, and models, let's dive into the heart of instructional coaching: coaching cycles. These structured processes are essential for helping teachers effectively integrate technology (or other practices) into their classrooms. These cycles are goal-oriented, data-driven, and reflective. When correctly implemented, coaching cycles ensure positive relationships and achieve results.

They also offer a framework for technology integration by identifying goals, learning and planning strategies, implementing and observing practices, reflecting on outcomes, and improving. Coaches can effectively support teachers in enhancing their instructional practices and improving student learning outcomes using educational technology.

Numerous coaching cycles are available; a quick online search will yield many options. It is also recommended that you collaborate with your team of EdTech coaches (if applicable) to develop a customized cycle for your school. When exploring coaching cycles, consider different authors' perspectives and insights. In this chapter, we'll introduce you to ASPIRE, one example of an educational technology coaching cycle.

 **Aimee**

The coaching cycle that you are about to review in the next section is just an example of one that you may be doing already. One day, though, I had an "aha" moment while sketching out my experiences as an educational technology coach (ETC) on a scrap paper for quick reference; I noted that the initials of the words I wrote spelled out the word ASPIRE. We love our acronyms in education, many of which change meaning from state to state!

As a green ETC, I stumbled through the coaching landscape, tripping over my assumptions and misconceptions. But with each misstep, I gained a deeper understanding of what effective coaching truly means. I'll never forget my early experiences as an ETC. I was so eager to help students that I overwhelmed teachers with advice. It was a humbling experience, but it taught me the importance of listening before speaking.

Through online coaching series, research, and countless experiences, I've learned that coaching isn't just about giving advice; it's about connecting with educators, understanding their needs, and supporting their growth.

When I first started coaching, I felt overwhelmed by the sheer number of things I needed to keep track of, especially because I was also teaching classes simultaneously. To stay organized, I created a detailed coaching log for each session to use as a roadmap. One of the most helpful sections in my coaching log was the "Goals" section. This allowed me to clearly define what we wanted to achieve together and track our progress over time. My coaching logs were like a living document, evolving and growing with each new session. They helped me stay focused, organized, and accountable.

There are many iterations of a coaching cycle, and I encourage you to discover the cycle that fits your consumption and needs. In a world of educational acronyms, I apologize for throwing yet another your way. Although this coaching cycle is nothing groundbreaking, please allow me to introduce you to ASPIRE.

Scan the QR code to make a copy of the ASPIRE Coaching Cycle Reflection Workbook. This personal reflection tool will help you grow professionally by reflecting on your experiences and insights. The workbook includes a collaborative coaching log you and your learner can use to navigate the coaching cycle together.

ASPIRE Coaching Cycle Reflection Workbook

Unleash the Power of the ASPIRE Coaching Cycle to Integrate Technology in Education

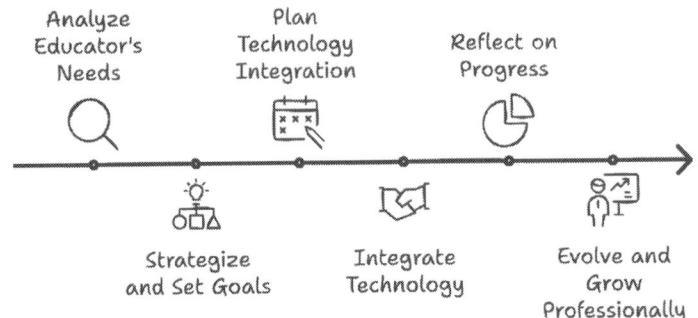

Let's explore each component of Aimee's example, ASPIRE, together! As you work through the coaching cycle with a colleague, you must be open and transparent about the process and how it will benefit both of you. This will help establish trust, eliminate inconsistencies, and strengthen your professional relationship.

If you're new to coaching, remember that the coaching cycle is inherently cyclical. Due to the dynamic nature of education, with its ever-changing challenges and constraints, the cycle often involves ongoing review and adjustment.

Analyze

The initial phase of the coaching cycle is to analyze an educator's needs and objectives. This foundational step ensures that the coaching process is tailored to their specific context, promoting effective on-demand professional development and growth. This ongoing process will involve identifying and addressing the educator's needs at various stages. As the coaching cycle begins, analyzing their needs helps build rapport, trust, and understanding of the educator's background knowledge. You can determine needs through general conversations, non-evaluative observations, surveys, questionnaires, and, if necessary, personality tests and skills inventories.

What have I learned about this through my experience during this phase? It's to meet your learners where they are. For example, if they are uncomfortable with the idea, don't plan on an informal observation to understand their curriculum. I learned this the hard way when trying to understand the dynamics of a teacher's classroom curriculum and how I could help. What I thought was an innocent endeavor was perceived as overbearing and judgmental. Through this experience, I evolved and learned that it is not about the formality of the process as much as it is about the human.

However, analyzing needs is essential to the process because you must understand what you will be working with before the cool stuff happens. Another way to look at it is that the educator you are working with is like the patient. You are the nurse who analyzes and may pinpoint the exact needs while the patient is in the second waiting room (because we all know they just moved the patient from the general waiting room to the exam room to wait longer).

You are attempting to discover why your patient is here—and if they have any medical past, they may have to help uncover future antidotes. You are analyzing. You are assessing. You are also anticipating any potential obstacles that may be in the way, such as the educator's fear of the unknown or lack of resources. You are also advocating thoughtfully for the use of educational technology integration. The analyze phase gives you a story. Once this phase is complete, you can proceed to the strategize phase.

Strategize

The strategize phase puts your story from the analysis phase into motion. One aspect of this phase is goal setting. Goal setting sparks meaningful discussions and gives us a clear target. It's like having a roadmap that guides and drives us forward. In later chapters, as you continue reading, we'll dive into creating SMART goals professionally, which is super important. In the coaching cycle, you will want to help educators set their own goals and decide how they can integrate educational technology into their lessons and develop a plan of action. The information you have gathered in the analyze phase can assist you in this endeavor.

But it doesn't stop there; keeping tabs on those goals is crucial. Regular check-ins, like scheduled sessions, will help you track progress, overcome challenges, and tweak the plans as needed. Sometimes, you might need to adjust the goals collaboratively based on how things are going and what's happening around you.

In this phase, you may also want to strategize and identify the resources you will need to succeed. This includes hardware (robotics, devices, etc.), software, and professional development opportunities, to name a few. Please also take the time to strategize how collaboration will look through the remainder of the phases (more on that to come).

 **Laurie**

Every year, I write down my goals for the coming year. They often are built off of where I left off the year before. I also have those who work for me write their goals for the year. These usually align with the program's goals but also focus on our professional development. For example, one goal was to create a library of professional learning opportunities.

We wanted to build resources, explore emerging technologies, expand our loaning program, and offer more significant support for our computer science standards rollout. From there, we kept a list of accomplishments. We created a website as a team and hosted over 100 workshops, webinars, and coaching cycles. We also presented at conferences, hosted cohorts, and expanded our knowledge of tech tools.

We were a part of this goal, but how we accomplished it varied based on our roles, experiences, opportunities, and knowledge. One of my team members focused on bringing nature and social emotional learning into the classrooms and his training. He hosted our STEM, EdTech, and SEL cohorts monthly, where he brought in vendors for demos, allowed for peer-to-peer learning, and cowrote a guidebook that suggested monthly activities to get students outside.

He added trail cams and 360 cameras to our loaning program. He shared his knowledge about our local wildlife with real skulls to teach about habitats, biology, and earth science in authentic interdisciplinary activities, including data collection, graphing, and scientific discovery. He showcased some of the group's projects on a global scale during the international student showcase in April of 2023. You can see his work in action by scanning the QR code.

Global Student Showcase

BOCES Book Kits

Another team member created book kits that combined literacy with computer science. She then presented these activities at local conferences and within our districts. We tied in our loaning program, allowing for rich, hands-on experiences. She researched and went through certification programs for emerging technology companies and served on the library council to build relationships and look for collaboration opportunities. Scan the QR code below to explore her work.

She also created weekly newsletters focused on the goals of the schools she served and showcased ways to integrate technology effectively. This team member spent much time in classrooms, making interdisciplinary and engaging activities to foster growth mindsets and students' excitement over learning.

As a team, we were able to not only meet the specific goal of building that library, but we were also able to put that library to use with all of our professional learning opportunities, coaching, modeling, and supporting of teachers and classrooms across our area and beyond. By having a clear goal, we could collect the data to see how well what we were building was working, offer feedback and support, and explore ways to move beyond the library and into practice. We celebrated a lot of success, which was especially evident in the smiles on the faces of students and teachers alike.

Plan

The plan phase of the coaching cycle focuses on preparing and planning the lesson you want to enhance the instruction/lesson/activity with the educator you are coaching. Your approach to preparation and planning may vary each time you coach, even if you've worked with the same person. Depending on the educator's comfort level and your level of comfort and expertise, you might do most of the preparation and planning alone, then present your findings and seek feedback.

You also want to strengthen, support, and share how the integration (or how technology can seamlessly be incorporated into the teaching and learning process) will work.

Alternatively, you can prepare and plan with the educator you are coaching. Either way, your ultimate goal is to set all parties up for success, including yourself—but please understand that failure is inevitable. As discussed briefly in the strategize phase, we encourage you to discuss how you will collaborate throughout this process. Allow Aimee to explain why:

Aimee

Collaboration is a powerful force that needs to be discussed during the coaching cycle. Collaboration is more than just working together; it's about embracing our differences, listening to diverse perspectives, and creating a space where everyone feels valued and empowered.

While we may instinctively think that collaboration should come naturally, it's a skill that requires practice and nurturing. From childhood to adulthood, we can learn and grow our ability to collaborate effectively. Educational institutions can play a crucial role in fostering these skills through more experiential learning and collaborative projects. And let's remember the power of play! Even as adults, engaging in activities that promote teamwork and creativity can help us develop stronger collaborative abilities.

So, let's make collaboration a cornerstone of our work and personal lives. By embracing diversity, listening with empathy, and fostering a supportive environment, we can achieve remarkable things together.

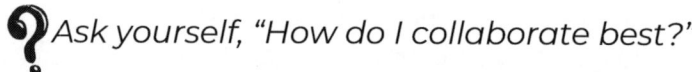

Ask yourself, "How do I collaborate best?"

For example, when working on a big project, I prefer to have time to process the task independently. I enjoy listening to others' viewpoints once I have processed my thoughts. I also need to collaborate and work on the project independently. When we regroup, everyone shares their accomplishments, thoughts, and ideas and supports each other with teachable moments. Through discussion, we make any necessary adjustments.

I've had experiences where people wanted to work together every step of the way, which was mentally taxing for me. I advocate for my needs, although someone once took it personally and said I knew nothing about collaboration. It hurt, but they didn't understand that meeting me halfway is a crucial step for effective collaboration.

So please, take that moment and ask yourself, "How do I collaborate best?"

However, my stance on my needs during a collaborative moment would change when I was coaching another educator. I considered what others might feel about collaboration during the strategize phase. I would ask, "How do you see us working together to get this off the ground?" Remember, collaboration is a two-way street. It's about finding common ground, respecting differences, and working together toward a shared vision. I would suggest to the educator that we approach the project with open minds and a willingness to learn from each other.

I also warned them that if we were doing any kind of research or creating items for integration and implementation during the plan phase, they would need to embrace the fact that I talk to myself a lot.

Once you have outlined the best course of action for an engaging technology-enhanced lesson, it's time to determine how technology integration will occur. After you've ensured the lesson is aligned with standards, good pedagogy, and instructional practices, the fun part is putting it into motion! Failure is an essential learning component regardless of how much you plan and prepare. In this phase, you will prepare. You will prioritize. You will be a partner.

Integration

Integration is hands down one of the best phases of the coaching cycle, as you both see your efforts come to light. At the same time, it can be a roller coaster of expectations, uncertainty, excitement, and failure. During this phase, you have several options for integrating the lesson. As noted above, I encourage you to have an open discussion about how you would consider carrying out the rollout or implementation of the lesson during the strategizing phase, as it will allow you to understand better the comfort level and needs and how you will collaborate.

How can you collaborate during the integration phase? Here are a few ways:

Modeling

In real time, modeling allows you to demonstrate specific teaching strategies, classroom management techniques, or instructional approaches. It also allows educators to see how instructional practices and methods are applied practically in a classroom setting. Most importantly, it gives educators a chance to gain confidence by observing the successful implementation of new techniques, making them more likely to try these methods themselves when they are comfortable doing so independently.

When modeling occurs, you and the educator discuss the lesson plan, objectives, and specific strategies and technologies you will model. This conversation ensures that the demonstration aligns with the educator's and students' goals, most of which should be predetermined during the coaching cycle's assessing needs and goals phase.

Modeling can take various forms, from live classroom modeling to a video recording where you prerecord a video of yourself teaching how to implement the lesson. You can also incorporate videos from the web from sites such as the Teaching Channel or Edutopia.

Edutopia Videos   Teaching Channel

Co-Teaching

Co-teaching involves both you and the educator actively participating in the delivery of instruction, providing a collaborative approach to teaching. This is usually best when the educator is comfortable doing so. You can provide in-the-moment support and feedback, which can help to refine and improve the educator's teaching practices on the spot. Please exercise caution when offering in-the-moment support and take a moment to set and define norms and expectations so feelings are not hurt.

Co-teaching models encompass a variety of approaches, including:

Station Teaching

In this model, one teacher assumes the role of the lead instructor while the other provides support and assistance to meet the diverse needs of students. This allows for a more flexible and personalized approach to teaching.

Parallel Teaching

Both teachers collaborate to deliver instruction to separate groups of students simultaneously, often in the same room. This approach enables more targeted and individualized instruction, catering to each group's specific learning preferences and needs.

Alternative Teaching

In this model, the classroom is organized into stations or centers, and each teacher is responsible for instructing students at different stations. Students rotate between stations and engage in various activities, creating a differentiated and dynamic learning experience.

Team Teaching

This approach involves teachers collaboratively delivering instruction to the entire class. Combining their expertise and sharing responsibility for the whole class can provide a comprehensive and cohesive learning experience, integrating different perspectives and teaching styles.

The Lone Ranger

This is where the educator, with your assistance, feels comfortable doing this alone with you in the background as a champion.

Remember that it is important to set clear expectations and guidelines on how the integration phase will look from beginning to end. Make sure to meet the individual you are supporting where they are.

# Reflect

Reflection is crucial in education. Taking the time and effort to do so requires discipline, understanding, and trust between colleagues. In this phase of the coaching cycle, self- and peer assessments and reflection are essential for growth and continuous improvement. Having structured protocols for the reflection phase can alleviate confusion and reduce anxiety. Reflection can be done by dialogue or by answering a series of questions.

To begin the reflection journey, gather feedback, observations, and notes from either yourself or the educator you worked with, collected before, during, and after the implemented lesson. Gather qualitative data by asking questions such as what went well, what didn't go well, why, how the students responded, and what you would do differently next time. This can be in the form of a conversation with someone as a note-taker or done using a form for data collection.

Various data types, beyond collective responses, can be used for data collection, which can be a good indicator of success or room for improvement and reflection. Collect data points, such as increased usage of a tech tool, engagement metrics of a tool, formative or summative data, or work samples, to provide solid talking points for evaluating the integration phase.

When it comes to data collection, it's essential to utilize a diverse range of data types, not just relying on collective responses from surveys or feedback forms. By broadening your approach, you can gain a more nuanced understanding of what is working well and where there might be opportunities for improvement or further reflection.

Moreover, incorporating both formative and summative assessment data can help gauge the impact of the technology on learning outcomes. Formative assessments, collected throughout the integration process, can inform adjustments and guide improvements, while summative assessments can provide a comprehensive overview of the tool's effectiveness once the integration period has concluded.

Videos are another great way to reflect on the integration phase if all parties are comfortable being recorded. Often, this requires vulnerability, but it is a courageous way to watch yourself for improvement. It provides opportunities for deep self-reflection and the ability to analyze all occurrences during the lesson.

Most importantly, scheduling this reflection piece to hold each of you accountable is important. Sometimes, when a lesson goes well, it is tempting to skip this step in its entirety. Please do not, as there is always room for improvement and growth. Reflection also provides closure.

Chapter two discussed how feedback loops are essential in the coaching cycle journey. Using feedback loops effectively in a coaching cycle, you can assist educators in reaching their full potential and developing the skills and knowledge they need to succeed. Ensure you meet or check in regularly to establish a healthy rapport with your coachee and be transparent throughout the process.

Don't know where to start with reflection? Scan the QR code for our Coaching Collaboration Notebook template to get you on your way! Once you scan the QR code, scroll to the end of the document to review the reflection questions.

Coaching
Collaboration
Notebook

 **Evolve**

Why is "evolve" in the ASPIRE coaching cycle? Because your professional growth is equally important here. This goes beyond the reflection within the coaching cycle and focuses more on your professional growth and goals. Evolve focuses on you. When you have completed a coaching cycle, take the time to self-reflect and analyze any gaps you need to address to help define your craft. Are there gaps in your learning and understanding? What personally made you open your eyes, or what went very well unexpectedly? What research, professional development opportunities, or professional learning networks can you participate in to assist you? As a bonus, this final closure step can be aligned with your professional goals, which we discuss in the next chapter.

Coaching cycles are more than just a process; they're a catalyst for transformation. They provide a structured framework that empowers teachers to integrate technology seamlessly into their classrooms. By setting clear goals, gathering valuable data, and reflecting on progress, we can promote a culture of continuous improvement.

Through coaching cycles, we build strong relationships, inspire innovation, and enhance student learning experiences. Remember, every phase is essential. Open communication and transparency are the keys to success. Let's embrace the power of coaching cycles and unlock the full potential of technology in our classrooms.

This chapter thoroughly examines the multifaceted components of coaching, encompassing standards, models, frameworks, and a comprehensive coaching cycle. Subsequent chapters will explore professional development, the seamless integration of educational technology, the art of effective goal setting, and an insightful analysis of the prevalent reasons behind coaching challenges and failures. Before we move on, please take a moment to reflect. Given the various coaching cycles and approaches discussed, how can you tailor your coaching style to best meet the unique needs and preferences of the educators you work with?

Chapter 7

Creating a Comprehensive EdTech Coaching Plan
~ Laying the Foundation ~

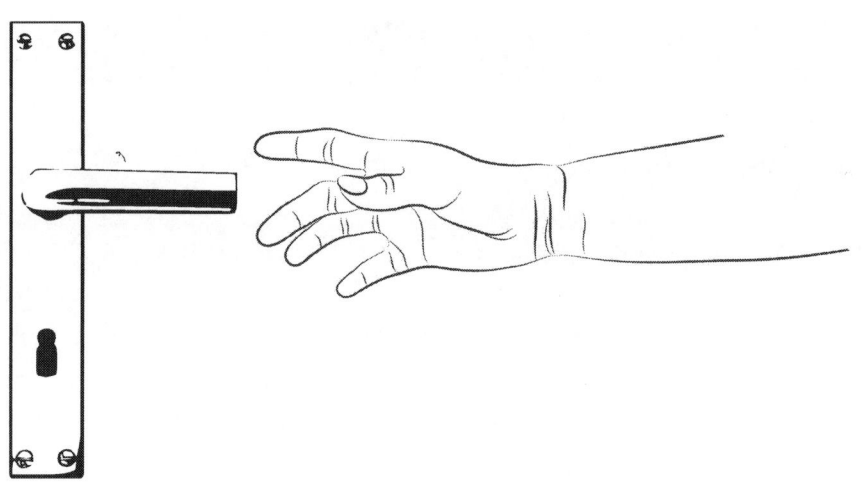

"The door handle is the handshake of the building."

—Juhani Pallasmaa (architect, author, and architectural theorist)

Constructing the Learning Environment: Integrating Technology Effectively

Let's explore what makes educational technology coaches truly exceptional. Beyond simply employing new teaching methods, you play a pivotal role in shaping instruction and curriculum across various subjects, from math and English to foreign languages and music. What distinguishes this role is the seamless integration of educational technology tools. With the vast array of tools available, even the tech-savvy can feel overwhelmed. And as educational technology constantly evolves, staying current can be a challenge. What will the next big trend be? And which tools are best suited for teachers at different skill levels?

If you're new to this, take a deep breath. The first thing to consider is what tools your school or district already provides. These tools have usually been vetted and received your district's stamp of approval. Understanding and obtaining various technology tool usage analytics is essential to know who uses them and how. Most educational technology tools provide some insights as to how they are being used, and you can gather rich data on engagement metrics, such as time spent on specific tools, frequency of use, and interactions with content.

Use a single sign-on service, such as Clever or ClassLink. These services can provide overall data across multiple apps and websites and give you information such as the frequency of application launches, time spent within applications, and most frequently used features. This data can help you understand the overall usage of educational tools across the school or district and how frequently teachers use different educational tools in their classrooms. Using usage data can provide an excellent stepping stone to assist your school's teachers (more on that later in this chapter).

To introduce new tools, you must take steps beforehand, such as understanding your state's student privacy laws and how the application collects, stores, and uses student data. For instance, in New York State, a law called EdLaw 2-d safeguards student data and privacy. This law ensures that software vendors take steps to protect student information. While these laws may seem overwhelming, it's essential to participate in the effort to safeguard student privacy. Please take a moment to familiarize yourself with your state's student data and privacy law. For more information on student privacy, please scan the QR code.

Protecting Student Privacy
U.S. Department of Education

When considering adding a new tool to your educational tool kit, also take a moment to carefully evaluate its potential benefits and drawbacks. Remember, sometimes less is more. Before introducing a shiny new tool, ask yourself if there's a similar one already in use. For example, Nearpod and Pear Deck aim to increase student engagement through interactive lessons. While each has its unique features, the core function is similar. If your school already uses Pear Deck effectively, adding a redundant tool might confuse teachers and create an unnecessary workload.

Educators often prefer tools that are not only user-friendly but also easily integrated into their curriculum. For this reason, it's crucial to consider ease of use and long-term sustainability when evaluating a technology tool. In addition, it's vital to ensure the application is accessible to students with various disabilities, including visual, auditory, or motor impairments.

On the technical side, it's essential to thoroughly review the minimum system requirements of new tech tools you're considering to guarantee compatibility with the school's infrastructure. Additionally, assessing the range of devices the application supports, such as computers, tablets, and smartphones, is crucial for seamless implementation across different platforms.

Aimee

I want to share a quick tip: When checking out new tech tools, I like to set up a quick meeting with the vendor and have them walk me through a tutorial. This way, I ensure I don't miss any cool features or ways to use the tool. This is also an excellent opportunity to get to know the company I'll be buying from and how they can support me in promoting their product, whether it's through offering professional development or monthly newsletters. I'm all about building a partnership!

Consider using a resource like Common Sense Media to assess a tool's value. This platform and similar ones offer reviews, usage guides, and information on student engagement, helping you make informed decisions. Ratings and reviews are also fantastic for gathering information. Often, these are reviews from parents, teachers, and kids who understand the app or website's content and features.

Technology Evaluation
Using Gemini

An alternative method to consider is leveraging technology evaluation tools to assess various software and tech solutions. A quick search on Google will provide you with numerous options to explore. Additionally, you can develop your evaluation criteria or seek support using generative AI systems. As an example, you can use Gemini or another AI tool to create a comprehensive evaluation based on your specific requirements and preferences. Scan the QR code to see an example using Gemini.

In addition, you can assess your educational technology tool against various educational models, including ISTE (International Society for Technology in Education), Triple E (Engage, Enhance, Extend), SAMR (Substitution, Augmentation, Modification, Redefinition), and TPACK (Technological Pedagogical Content Knowledge) as discussed in chapter five.

For more information on AI, scan this QR code to access our AI resources.

ArchiTech: Laying the Foundation for EdTech Coaching AI Tools Wakelet

Tip from Aimee

When I was in an instructional technology "coaching role," I had the opportunity to increase awareness of our school's awesome educational technology tools. These tools weren't getting the love and attention they deserved, so I took a two-pronged approach. I wanted to showcase our technology and connect to the curriculum. As a newbie in the school, I also focused on building relationships.

So, what did I do? Based on teachers' schedules, I offered short 10-minute PD sessions in the morning and again in the afternoon. These bite-size sessions focused on specific skills, applications, or ways to use technology in the classroom. In addition, I teamed up with teachers who were already rocking these tools in their classrooms. Together, we conducted the 10-minute PD sessions where they demonstrated how they used the technology, and I provided technical support and quick tips.

This approach increased participation in the PD sessions and helped build strong partnerships with educators already utilizing the technology. I always emphasized to the teachers that they were the experts in their classrooms, and my role was to guide them. I tailored the PD sessions to reflect this belief.

Remember that no matter your role in education, your ultimate customer is the student. Therefore, it is extremely important to evaluate the software based on student engagement, ease of use, and accessibility. Speaking of roles, let's now shift to rolling out a plan.

Keeping the Customer Happy by Customizing a Rollout Plan

Many factors must be considered when planning the rollout of a new technology tool. First, defining the rollout goals using specific, measurable, achievable, relevant, and time-bound (SMART) targets to track progress and success is essential (we visit SMART goals later in this chapter). Once the goals are set, establish a timeline with key milestones, tasks, and responsibilities for all stakeholders involved. Often, it is best to form a committee to ensure all voices are heard and that there is continuity in the execution of the plan.

It is recommended that a communication plan be developed to inform stakeholders (teachers, students, parents, and administrators) about the new tool, its benefits, and how to use it effectively. Use various communication channels like emails, newsletters, announcements, and social media to reach all stakeholders.

To ensure successful implementation of the new tool, carefully planning how to train others in your school is essential. If the training is conducted by someone other than you, designate specific individuals responsible for the training sessions. Consider choosing experienced staff members with a solid understanding of the tool and practical teaching abilities. A comprehensive support system will also assist users after the training. This support system should encompass technical support, readily available troubleshooting resources, and ongoing professional development opportunities to help users continuously enhance their skills with the new tool.

Another recommendation is to offer training sessions in various formats, such as workshops, webinars, online tutorials, or job-embedded professional development. Play is an integral part of learning; it provides opportunities for teachers and students to practice using the tool in a simulated or real-world setting. Also, when offering ongoing support and resources to help users learn and adapt to the tool, embed the UDL principles we reviewed in chapter four.

Often, it's a good idea to begin with a small-scale pilot of the new technology. This will involve selecting a group of teachers and students to test the tool in a carefully controlled environment. Gathering feedback from these pilot participants is crucial for identifying potential issues or areas needing improvement. This feedback will enable you to make necessary adjustments to ensure the technology meets the users' needs.

Remember our discussion above about usage data? Well, it's back. At the final stage, it is important to consistently utilize data and analytics to monitor the tool's usage and effectiveness. Gathering feedback from teachers, students, and administrators is essential to comprehensively evaluating the tool's impact and understanding any learning gaps in the new software. Based on the insights gathered from this feedback and data, be ready to make necessary adjustments to the rollout plan to ensure its effectiveness.

By carefully considering these factors and implementing a comprehensive rollout plan, schools can successfully integrate new technology tools into their teaching and learning environments. Effective planning and execution will ensure these tools enhance student learning, improve teaching practices, and support school goals. Remember, the ultimate success of any technology rollout depends on its alignment with the school's vision and the active participation of all stakeholders.

Constructing a Roadmap: Aligning EdTech with Educational Goals

Goal setting is an essential and crucial part of your role as an educational technology coach that should not be overlooked. It's not just about having a direction; it's also about setting the right goals to maximize your efforts. Setting your professional (and personal) goals allows you to internalize the goal-setting regime better, making you more effective when coaching others and helping them with their goals.

There are many frameworks to assist you on your goal-setting journey, such as Simon Sinek's The Golden Circle, Objectives and Key Results (OKRs), and Backward Goals. One of the most popular and widely used is the SMART goals framework. The SMART goals framework, which stands for specific, measurable, achievable, relevant, and time-bound, is a powerful tool in goal setting as it provides a very structured recipe for moving things forward. By aligning your goals with the SMART criteria, you can ensure they are clear, achievable, and actionable, leading to effective outcomes in your role.

Let's take a closer look at how you can apply the SMART goal framework to your role as an educational technology coach.

Specific

As a coach, you likely have many responsibilities, from helping teachers integrate technology into their lessons to working with administrators to develop technology plans. When setting practical goals, being specific about what you want to achieve is important. This might mean setting a goal to help a certain number of teachers incorporate a new tool into their instruction or to develop a new professional development program for your school and how to embrace and incorporate AI, for example. This goal may be more personal or professional. Suppose you aim to achieve a certification such as a Google Innovator or Microsoft Certified Educator (MCE). Whatever your goal is, make sure to take time to reflect on how it will impact not only you professionally but also your school community.

Measurable

Measurability is also key to creating effective goals. By setting clear metrics for success, you can track your progress and make adjustments as needed. For example, you might set a goal to increase the number of teachers using Nearpod to capture formative assessments by 20% by the end of the school year.

Achievable

Achievability is another important factor to consider. While it's important to set challenging goals, it's also important to ensure they are within reach. Setting goals that are too difficult to achieve can be demotivating, whereas setting goals that are too easy can lead to complacency. Consider your resources, skills, and time constraints to ensure your goals are achievable. In other words, make sure the goal you set is just right. May we also recommend using planners, digital calendars, reminders, or goal-setting apps to assist you on your way!

Relevant

Relevance is also important when setting goals. Your professional goals should align with your overall mission as an educational technology coach and help you move closer to your larger objectives. For example, if your goal is to help teachers integrate technology into their lessons, this should be aligned with your school's broader goals around technology integration. Discuss your goals with various stakeholders to ensure they align with the greater good.

Time-bound

Finally, having time-bound goals gives you a clear deadline to work toward, which can help keep you motivated and focused. Setting a specific time frame for achieving your goals allows you to break down your work into manageable chunks and ensure that you stay on track.

Aimee

Every year, as the clock strikes midnight on the eve of January 1, many of us set "New Year's Resolutions." A great example of this is weight loss. If you're a gym goer then you probably notice how the gym becomes packed starting January 2 (because we all give ourselves a holiday buffer day), and by March, attendance fizzles. We don't do this intentionally. In fact, I would like to say most of us drop our "resolutions" because they are unrealistic, or we have unrealistic expectations of ourselves.

As a driven person, setting goals is essential for achieving my dreams. It's a strategy I've used to excel in my career, and it's helped me stay motivated in my personal life. For example, when I decided to pursue my second master's degree in Educational Leadership, I didn't just say, "I'll do it someday." I set specific milestones, defined a clear goal, and aligned it to my why. I broke down chunks for what I wanted to have completed by when, and I mapped out how I was going to achieve this goal. This approach keeps me accountable and motivated.

I also apply this strategy to my personal goals. As a runner (I call myself that because I can move in a forward motion) who's always looking to improve, I set specific race goals with clear timelines. This helps me track my progress and celebrate my achievements.

So, as we approach the new year, consider setting SMART goals for yourself. Make sure they're specific, measurable, achievable, relevant, and time-bound. It might just be the key to achieving your dreams, as it has been for me.

As an educational technology coach, you can use the SMART framework or others that fit your needs to set goals and create actionable objectives that help you achieve your goals and support your school's broader mission of technology integration. Aside from setting goals, you will assist others while working through the coaching cycle. First, let's practice setting your own professional goals.

Setting your professional goals as an educational technology coach

The following section will examine how you can apply the SMART method to your goal-setting needs. This is a great time to dive into the goal-setting resource we provide or simply have a notebook and pen ready to jot down notes as you follow along. If you chose the former, now is your time to scan the QR code, make a copy of the resource, and follow along as we dissect each section to give you a framework for setting your goals.

SMART Goal Action Plan

Specific

So, what do you want to improve upon? Or are you just thinking about being an educational tech coach? What do you need to learn to be more successful? Is this goal relevant to your role, and can you achieve it within a reasonable amount of time? While we are asking you all these questions, please take a moment to dive back and forth between our questions and your reflections in the SMART Goal Action Plan or on your own.

As you brainstorm your thoughts and ideas on creating your own SMART goal, please allow our example to help guide you to your ultimate goal.

Example:
"I want to improve technology integration in classrooms to enhance student learning."

Now, let's take a moment to ensure specificity by brainstorming and answering the following questions:

- What do you want to accomplish?
- Why is this goal important?
- Who is involved?
- What is the location? For example, is this an online course you are teaching? Or if you are in a district, is it within a particular building?
- Which resources or limits are involved?

Once you have selected your professional goal, it's time to devise an action plan. What are the steps you will take to achieve your goal?

- Are there professional development opportunities that interest you? List them, along with their dates and locations, and what you will accomplish there.
- Are there professional learning networks (PLNs) you can actively join to gain the support, knowledge, and expertise you need to help build your capacity and offer support? Take the time to research and join them.
- How can you keep abreast of the latest trends, research, and innovations in educational technology? Are there blogs and journals you can read or affiliations you can join to assist you?
- What certifications do you want to participate in to enhance your skill set?

Measurable

This is sometimes the overlooked part of goal setting. We need data to determine if we are on track and successful. Think about it: How are you going to measure the success of your goals and be able to identify indicators of progress and completion? Ask yourself:

- How will I measure the results in quantity, frequency, or quality?
- How many individuals will I impact?
- How will I know when it is accomplished?

This is the perfect time to reflect and determine the measurable part of your goal!

Did you come up with a few key data points for your goal? Excellent. Now, let's take a moment to discuss the types of data we can use to ensure we are reaching our goal: quantitative versus qualitative data.

Quantitative data is all about numbers—it can be measured or counted. We can express hard data in numbers, statistics, or measurements. Regarding educational technology, quantitative metrics can help us track how much teachers and students use the tools we've trained them on. We can measure the number of logins, time spent using the tools, how often they're used, and the types of activities being performed.

Qualitative data is about capturing the rich, descriptive details that can't be easily measured. It's like diving into a story—through words, images, and observations, we explore the context, meaning, and experiences behind the data. Imagine chatting with educators, students, and other key players, using surveys, interviews, and focus groups to uncover their thoughts on technology integration. We're talking about their insights, the ups and downs they've faced, and their visionary ideas for improvement. It's all about understanding the human side of data!

Qualitative data can involve conducting classroom assessments to gauge the effectiveness of teachers' use of technology in their teaching. For example, you can observe students' interaction with technology, their engagement, and the overall impact on their learning experiences. You can also create feedback mechanisms, such as surveys, through which teachers and students can continually provide input on the usability, effectiveness, and relevance of technology tools and resources. Just keep in mind that qualitative data can sometimes be subjective.

Here's an example for you:

"I will conduct four workshops, one per quarter, and gather feedback from at least 80% of the participants to measure effectiveness."

Please refer to your notes and add how you will collect the data you want to measure.

Achievable

When working toward your goal, consider the potential challenges and obstacles you might encounter. Take a moment to think about the resources available at your school and how you can leverage them to achieve your goal. Ensure that the goal is realistic and attainable by considering your schedule in and out of work and considering how to overcome any potential constraints to make it happen.

Here's an example:

"I have access to the school's professional development room and can allocate time during professional development days to conduct these workshops."

Please take the time to brainstorm on this part. Ask colleagues, family, and friends for advice, primarily if part of achieving your goal will happen outside your workday.

Relevant

We don't typically set goals that are not relevant to us. For example, if you have a fear of water, a goal to become a professional scuba diver may not only be unachievable but also irrelevant. You want to ensure that your goal will enrich your school building or district and you professionally. Confirm that the goal aligns with other objectives and is worthwhile by communicating your goal with the district and/or building leaders and colleagues. Think to yourself: Does this seem worthwhile? Is this the right time to set this goal? Does this goal match other efforts/needs of my institution?

Example:
"Enhancing technology use in classrooms aligns with the school's initiative to incorporate more digital learning tools."

Please take the time to align your goal with any district/school/classroom technology initiatives or think about how your goal will be relevant in excelling in your career. Jot down your ideas!

Time-bound

This is how you will stay on track. Think about when you want to accomplish your professional goal and the timeline for each actionable item. It is recommended to time this out accordingly, as you can properly align your goal with professional development opportunities, workshops, and other learning initiatives. Define a clear timeline, consider when you can accomplish it, what you can achieve by a specific date, and how to start today!

Example:
"I will complete all workshops by the end of the school year, with one workshop scheduled each marking quarter."

At first, you may sketch out a general brainstorming session for your timeline. As you collect everything you will need to accomplish this goal, tighten in on specific dates to hold yourself accountable, using whatever tool (digital or not) helps you along your way.

As you walked through the development of a SMART goal, you may have noticed we provided you with examples along the way! In summary, the overall SMART goal, taken from the example, is: "I will conduct four workshops by the end of the school year for teachers to improve their use of interactive technology tools in their lessons, gathering feedback from at least 80% of participants to measure effectiveness."

SMART Goal Action Plan

Please refer to the SMART Goal Action Plan to further dive into planning your professional goals. You can access the template by scanning the QR code.

As an educational technology coach, setting professional goals is vital in driving personal and organizational growth. By applying the SMART framework and creating actionable objectives, you can make significant strides in supporting technology integration within your schools. Through continuous learning, active participation in professional development opportunities and networks, and staying updated with the latest trends in educational technology, you can enhance your skill set and contribute effectively to your school's mission.

By measuring success through quantitative and qualitative metrics, you can continually assess your progress and adapt your strategies to achieve their goals. Once you dive into this chapter, you will become familiar with how to use the tools from this section to succeed in working with teachers. Practice makes perfect, right?

Chapter 8

Design Thinking Process
~ Don't Just Build It, Design It ~

"I am still learning."

—Michelangelo (sculptor, painter, architect, and poet)

Design Thinking

The Design Thinking Process (DTP) is a user-centered, iterative problem-solving approach that emphasizes understanding users' (customers') needs, generating innovative ideas, and testing solutions.

IDEO Design Thinking History

The Design Thinking Process emerged from architecture and industrial design in the 1960s and 1970s. It was popularized by David Kelley, Tim Brown of IDEO, and Roger Martin. This methodology evolved into a structured approach to problem-solving and innovation. To learn more about IDEO, please scan the QR code.

Design thinking can be used in education to design curricula and create student-centered learning experiences. Problem-based learning, which uses design thinking processes and classroom innovation, encourages students to tackle real-world problems. Design thinking can also aid in redesigning classroom environments to enhance learning and collaboration.

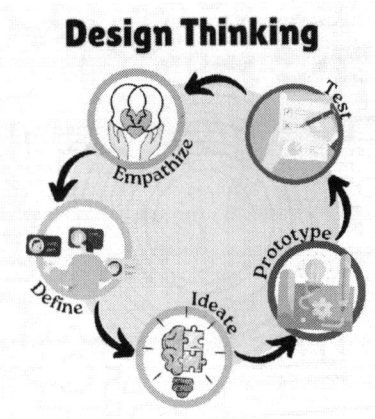

The Design Thinking Process (DTP) promotes critical thinking and nurtures creativity among students, educators, and coaches by guiding them through various stages, including empathy, definition, ideation, prototyping, and testing. By incorporating DTP as a coaching cycle, coaches can foster a deeper understanding of challenges and develop effective solutions through structured exploration and innovation.

At the same time, design thinking nurtures creativity by encouraging divergent thinking, hands-on experimentation, and iterative innovation. Similarly, in the empathy stage, understanding user needs inspires creative solutions tailored to real-world problems. The define stage encourages students to frame problems from new perspectives, sparking innovative approaches. Ideation fosters an environment where generating a wide range of ideas without immediate judgment and allows creativity to thrive. Prototyping engages students, educators, and coaches in practical creativity, turning abstract concepts into tangible prototypes. Finally, the testing stage prompts continuous creative problem-solving as students refine their prototypes based on feedback, leading to iterative improvements and innovative solutions.

But what does this mean for you as a coach?

Using the DTP as a Coaching Cycle

Helping educators navigate the Design Thinking Process involves collaboratively walking through a structured approach to improve the educators' teaching practices and effectively integrate technology in the classroom. This nonlinear, iterative process typically consists of five phases: empathize → define → ideate → prototype → test. And much like how individuals use this innovative process in the business world, each phase of the process in education has its unique place to enhance creative and critical thinking.

What is so powerful about using the Design Thinking Process while coaching is that the educators you work with will understand the value of iteration and deep creative thinking as they live the process with you. For more on how the Design Thinking Process can be used with teachers, scan the QR code to check out this video.

How to Conduct Design Thinking Workshop DavidLeeEdTech

Before we explore how the Design Thinking Process can be used in the classroom, let's see how you can use the process with educators while coaching. While these are two parallel topics, they're both ways of looking at a coaching framework.

Empathize

Remember this key point: Empathy involves comprehending educators' and students' experiences, challenges, and needs.

3 Ways to Develop Empathy in the Design Thinking Process Education Elements

Empathy is vital for building relationships and trust. However, understanding how to be empathetic can be tricky—especially for kids—since it requires them to set aside their feelings, beliefs, and biases to see how someone else experiences something. Scan the QR code to watch an Education Elements video on this topic.

 **Aimee**

Here's a lighthearted example to illustrate this point:

Imagine both of us drinking a soda (we call it "pop" in Western New York). Although we are drinking the same type of soda with the same ingredients—heck, it even came from the same bottle—we most likely will have entirely different experiences. I will find it too sweet and the fizz annoying, while you might down it like it's water, wanting more. I might think you're crazy for your love of sugary treats and look at you with disgust. You might be perplexed by my disgusted look and my lack of empathy for your love of soda. We will then have a disagreement about whether it is called "pop" or "soda."

So, to be genuinely empathetic, I would have to set aside my feelings and bias with the soda and, without judgment, relate your perspective and your appreciation of your love for soda.

The Design Thinking Process provides an authentic and practical approach to developing empathy for students, educators, and yourself. Digital Promise (scan the QR code to access the resource) offers an excellent resource called "Building Empathy | Learner Variability Project for the Adult Learner," which includes various tools to assist adult learners in creating an empathetic environment.

Building Empathy
Digital Promise

As a coach, you can build upon your empathetic behavior by conducting interviews and observations to gain insights from teachers and students. You can also use empathy maps (as illustrated throughout Digital Promise) to visualize users' thoughts, feelings, and experiences. Finally, you can shadow teachers in the classroom to understand their daily routines and challenges.

As a coach, having empathy is a powerful tool. We all know the famous quote from Marvel Comics' Spiderman: "With great power comes great responsibility." Empathy in coaching helps you understand your learners and their vulnerabilities, making you a better coach. Empathy lets you grasp your clients' (or educators') needs and feelings when using the Design Thinking Process to solve a defined problem during your coaching cycle.

Define

So, what's the problem?

In the define stage, you will clearly articulate the problem or challenge based on insights gathered during the empathize phase. This is the opportunity to understand the information and identify key pain points and opportunities for improvement.

Using "How Might We" Questions to Ideate on the Right Problems

During this phase, you will collaborate to develop problem statements that focus on specific, actionable issues. One effective approach is to use "How Might We" questions to articulate the challenge in a positive, solution-oriented manner. Are you interested in learning how to craft effective "How Might We" questions? Take a moment to scan the QR code and read Maria Rosala's article "Using 'How Might We' Questions to Ideate on the Right Problems" from the Nielsen Norman Group.

As a coach, you play a crucial role in the define phase. You can leverage this phase to build a trusting relationship with the individual you are coaching, using authentic dialogue to identify a problem to solve. This phase offers the opportunity to gain a deeper understanding of the individual, uncovering underlying meanings, clarifying misconceptions, and setting the stage for a productive path forward.

Mural Learning

Mural is a visual collaboration tool that assists teams in brainstorming, ideating, and collaborating on projects. It is an excellent addition to your EdTech tools to explore. Scan the QR code to learn more.

Ideate

In the ideation phase, you will generate ideas and potential solutions for the defined problem.

A great way to tackle the ideation phase is to facilitate brainstorming sessions with educators to encourage creative thinking. Use mind mapping, sketching, and SCAMPER to expand idea generation. SCAMPER (Substitute, Combine, Adapt, Modify, Put to another use, Eliminate, Reverse) is a creative thinking technique used to help individuals or teams generate new ideas or solve problems by applying different prompts to existing products, services, or processes. For more information and assistance on the SCAMPER process and other techniques, scan the QR code to visit this resource using Edutopia.

5 Techniques to Promote Divergent Thinking Edutopia

As a coach, your role in the ideation phase is pivotal. It's the perfect opportunity to foster collaboration and diverse perspectives. This approach encourages out-of-the-box thinking, leading to exploring unconventional solutions and new approaches to integrating technology into education. Ultimately, this can lead to more engaging and effective teaching and learning experiences.

Prototype

In the prototype phase, you will bring selected ideas to life by creating tangible representations to explore their feasibility.

This is a wonderful time to sketch lesson ideas; plan long-term, meaningful projects utilizing technology, and create examples if none exist. During this phase, you will be a valuable thought partner as you work side by side with the individual or group you are coaching. This is also a great opportunity to use AI to assist you on your prototype journey.

Test

During the testing phase of the Design Thinking Process, you get the chance to gather feedback and improve solutions by assessing prototypes with users. This is the perfect opportunity to try "prototypes" (aka lessons, new technologies, etc.) on a small scale in the classroom, observe their impact, and gather feedback from educators and students through surveys, interviews, and observations.

Take time to analyze the results and identify strengths, weaknesses, and areas for improvement. Remember, the Design Thinking Process is not linear but iterative, and the testing phase often leads to refining the prototype based on feedback and continuing testing until the solution is optimized. Coaches support educators in evaluating the effectiveness of their prototypes through structured feedback and reflection sessions.

Aimee

Quick tip by yours truly. One way that I would love to prototype and test either new technologies or curriculum (that I wrote or used) was to introduce this to a small group of students in a club. Even as an ETC, I ran several clubs with students. Why? To test and prototype—and to stay relevant if I was not also teaching a class. Running a club, even if it is during the day for 20 minutes during a lunch period for students, is an awesome, risk-free way for you to prototype and test out new stuff!

The iterative Design Thinking Process ensures that technology integration is effective and sustainable. By incorporating the Design Thinking Process, instructional technology coaches can empower educators to adopt a user-centered approach to problem-solving, encouraging innovation and improving the overall educational experience.

Turnkeying the Design Thinking Process

As an educational technology coach, you can turn the Design Thinking Process and guide educators through understanding and implementing the methodology, leveraging technology to enhance each stage—a fantastic way to bring the Design Thinking Process through workshops and professional development. By offering a variety of workshops and professional development sessions, you can effectively support educators in integrating the Design Thinking Process into their teaching practices.

During workshops, you can break down the principles of design thinking and its benefits in education, such as enhancing critical thinking, creativity, and empathy. Workshops can start with a simple introduction to the Design Thinking Challenge, sparking excitement and inspiration. Make sure to build in a time when educators can engage in hands-on activities to experience each stage of the process, keeping them engaged and motivated. Providing clear examples of how educators can use

the Design Thinking Challenge in the classroom and connecting the hands-on experiences will allow educators to feel what it is like to be a student going through this process.

8 Steps to Implementing Design Thinking in Your Classroom
Common Sense Media

For inspiration on how to use the Design Thinking Process in the classroom (and inspiration for including any examples and methods in your workshop or professional development), scan the QR codes to check out these resources.

A massive component of the Design Thinking Process is understanding our customers. And by customers, we mean not only the educators we work with but also the students we inadvertently shape. First, we examined how the Design Thinking Process could be used linearly or in place of a coaching cycle. Then, we looked at how you can coach educators on using this process in their classrooms, especially STEM-based or project-based learning classrooms. Finally, we will look at some educational technology tools you can use.

What Is Design Thinking, and How Can It Be Used in Classroom Teaching?
Richard James Rogers

Using EdTech in the Design Thinking Process

Incorporating educational technology into the Design Thinking Process can streamline activities, enhance collaboration, and make the process more efficient. Now that you have an understanding of what the DTP is, here are some ideas on how you can use technology for each stage:

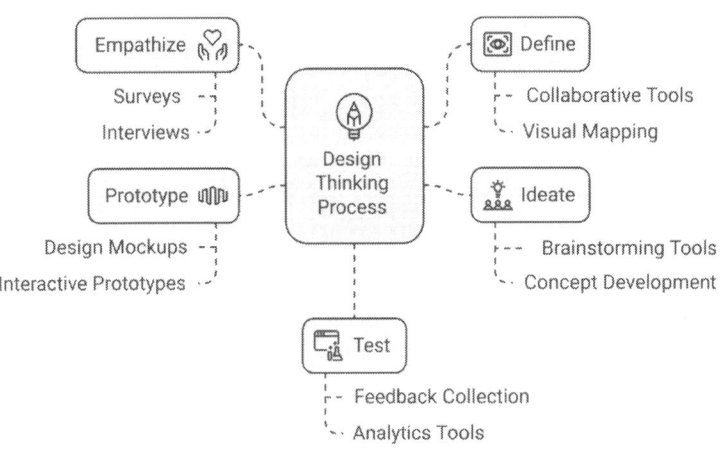

Wakelet Collection of Design Thinking Tech Tools You Could Use

Check out specific tools by scanning this QR code.

Integrating technology into the Design Thinking Process significantly improves efficiency and effectiveness across all stages. Digital tools are crucial in facilitating data collection, fostering collaboration, aiding visualization, enabling rapid prototyping, and supporting thorough testing. Ultimately, the infusion of technology makes the Design Thinking Process more dynamic and adaptable, enhancing its applicability across different contexts and scenarios.

The Design Thinking Process offers a powerful framework for educational technology coaches to empower educators and foster innovation. By guiding educators through the stages of empathy, defining, ideating, prototyping, and testing, coaches can cultivate a culture of creativity, critical thinking, and problem-solving. Through workshops, professional development, and the strategic integration of technology, coaches can equip educators with the skills and tools to transform their teaching practices and create engaging, student-centered learning experiences. As educational technology continues to evolve, the Design Thinking Process remains a valuable approach for driving innovation and improving educational outcomes.

Chapter 9

Coaching Educators for Growth
~ Adaptable and Transformable Architecture ~

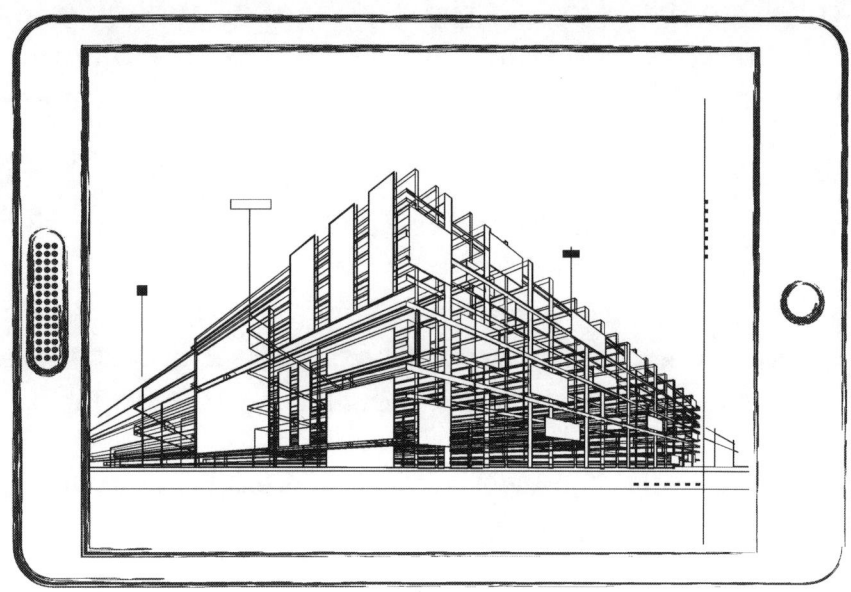

"You have to really believe not only in yourself; you have to believe that the world is actually worth your sacrifices."

—Zaha Hadid (architect)

When we first introduced ourselves to you in this book, we showcased how we tackle creativity. For Laurie, creativity is separate from real artistic talent, and for Aimee, creativity is as vital as the air she breathes. How about you? What are your feelings about creativity? Are you more like Laurie, looking for outlets for creativity, or Aimee, where creativity is just a part of who you are? These are important questions to ask as we explore the designing portion of coaching. Here, we are talking about how you organize and create professional learning opportunities, take advantage of hallway conversations, design learning materials, and communicate with others about your passion.

Before diving into creating meaningful PD, we need to discuss engagement. If you ask any educator who hosts PD sessions what's required for success, the words that you'll hear the most are that it needs to be "fun" and "engaging." This is also true when you think about what you want your students to say about your lessons in the classroom. But what is engagement, and how can we be sure we engage in the right ways?

Triple E Framework

Earlier in the book, we talked about the work of Liz Kolb and her Triple E framework. She talks about engagement and what it means to use research-based strategies. If you didn't take the time to explore her resources, this is a good time to do so before discussing creativity and how it relates to engagement.

Beyond just technology engagement, we will explore ways to measure engagement in general.

Measuring Engagement

Let's discuss ways to see and measure engagement. While this might not be an exhaustive list, it will help you consider ways to gauge whether your participants are interested in what you are presenting and think of ways to increase engagement in your coaching interactions. This is closely tied to our discussion of feedback loops in chapter two, as engagement is a massive part of what you will measure with feedback.

 Emotional

When you ask for feedback as a coach or a mentee, emotion may be tied to it. Think about the subject you struggled with the most in school. Now imagine being asked to teach a lesson on that topic and be observed around how you did in that lesson—you probably have some powerful emotions tied to it. This can result in the feedback you give is less than optimal because of the emotional baggage that the subject carries for you. This can also be true for coaching feedback, especially when you are coaching teachers who may not want to be coached but are being directed to be by the administration. If you feel your feedback is related to emotions, it's a good idea to reopen that feedback loop and listen.

Accessibility

Whether you're coaching a team or an individual, consider what accommodations will be needed. Much of this information can be gathered through the listening portion of the feedback process. However, it can also involve the teacher's access to support when needed and the materials necessary for their success.

If the people you are coaching hit a roadblock and need help getting what they need, they may become frustrated and disengaged. They will say they need clarification, or they might just refuse to participate in this coaching cycle. Their motivation may dip because they feel lost or unable to understand what is expected of them. This feeling of helplessness may make them withdraw and stop putting in effort. You will end up with inequitable results and a large achievement gap between them, you, and their fellow teachers.

Cognitive

Think about the mental load teachers bear and all the decisions they have to make in a typical day. The amount of mental processes we need to gain knowledge and understanding is astronomical, especially when this is added to our daily burdens. In a good feedback loop, we will look at cognition as a multifaceted approach that helps with learning. This learning could be new information or a shift in how the information is used. When thinking about educational technology, we need to add on our ability to reason and problem-solve since technology is constantly changing. We need to be able to determine which tool is the most effective for the learning objective, and we need to be able to solve problems as they arise.

A strong feedback loop will allow us to keep those lines of communication open to support this difficult work. Perception is one of the most significant barriers to the feedback loop. We must consider how we are perceived and how our content is perceived. We also want the new learning to stick.

Cognitive processes are complex and constantly changing in the educational world. For example, let's say you wanted to learn a new technology tool. You would first hear about the tool and maybe ask someone about it or navigate to the site to take a look. You must hold on to this new information and determine how you might leverage that tool. This includes remembering the name of the tool, the key features, and how it can be used. Once you have practiced using the tool, you will shift this information to your long-term memory for future retrieval.

In this case, it means making connections to your content or other tools that do similar things. You may analyze the layout and functionalities of the new tool and then determine if this tool is something that fills a need or solves a problem. For some, obtaining professional learning on the tool, watching online tutorials, or experimenting can help cement their understanding. Throughout this process, your cognitive load engages in metacognition, which means thinking about your own thinking. You monitor your learning, reflect on what works and doesn't, and adjust as needed. The cognitive process needs to work for engagement to be sustainable.

Technology Use

Let's say you want to survey your teachers' understanding of a new reading program. To fill out the survey, they need to download a new app, create an account, answer some basic questions, watch a short video clip, and then respond to some open-ended questions. The whole process takes about 30 minutes to complete. You give this survey to five people to test it out. One person fills out the form without any issue. Another hits a few stumbling blocks and sends you a few emails for help, but eventually completes the form. The third one fills out about half the survey and then can't get the video to load and gives up. The fourth person refuses to download the app, and the fifth one deletes the email without even trying because there were too many confusing steps.

In this scenario, technology was the barrier to success. It had nothing to do with what you were looking to learn; instead, the frustration of the tools caused the issue. You will often encounter this barrier and must be prepared when asking for engagement within the feedback loop.

Social Connotations

Take a moment and picture your classroom with all your students. They are all looking up at you, waiting for you to tell them what they are doing today. At the same time, think about what you know about each student. Some are probably hungry because of food insecurities, others are fighting sleepiness because of late-night gaming or stress, and others are anxious because a friend texted them something they are worried about.

No student in your class is fully engaged at that moment; the students are dealing with their social situations while trying to bring you focus. But if you have done the work in your class to create those connections and ensure that your students' well-being is at the forefront of everything you do, then you might be able to find the right balance between the task at hand and all the other things students deal with.

The same can be said for coaching. When looking at your staff, your team, or your coworkers, each has their social considerations that influence what they are capable of at that moment. One might be dealing with an ailing parent, another with pain from an injury or age, or maybe they are worried about their children or students for one hundred different reasons. When you are considering their reaction to the feedback you are offering, you have to take into account their anxiety, their perceptions, and their actual ability to focus.

Building Engagement

The best strategies to overcome these social barriers to increase engagement and participation are fairly simple. The first is to build a structure. This can be an agenda, an outline, guidelines, or even a shared space to air frustrations. If your participants have clear guidelines and expectations, they will feel more comfortable participating. Remember, the idea of learning styles has been debunked and there are preferences that we all feel. You may prefer to work in small groups, while others would rather work independently. Another person might be more comfortable leading a training versus being in a kindergarten classroom. We need to honor each person's preferences and encourage growth in other areas.

When beginning the coaching cycle, start small. Have participants each set small SMART goals for themselves and the group. Add check-in dates and explain how you will measure that success. Embrace positivity. Even when challenged with negative thoughts or comments, try to steer the conversations to more realistic self or group affirmations. Think of positive "I" and "we" statements that will help keep the feedback loop open and uplifting.

Keep It Simple

This is an excellent time to remember some of the basics. Relationships matter. If we were to do a word exploration of this book, we would guess that "relationships" is the most used word in the book. Nothing else can fall into place if you don't work on fostering them. While sometimes your coaching cycle is short, listening and offering support for every situation is still important, whether it's one-on-one training or large group presentations. It's also important to focus on the growth. Make sure you take moments to showcase the wins, no matter how small.

 Self-Regulation

Self-regulation plays a crucial role in overcoming the social aspects that hinder engagement. We must consider the other aspects of engagement and how well our coping mechanisms can help or hinder each situation. If we cannot self-regulate, then our participation will be diminished because of the anxiety we feel in each situation; it's too difficult to focus and process. This goes for both you as the coach and for those you are coaching.

Bring back the focus to the goals and small wins that a feedback loop can support to stay motivated and on task. Work on self-regulation skills by explicitly teaching emotional regulation, goal setting, and self-reflection in your feedback loops. This will save a ton of time and foster more success. You want those you coach to be independent and self-directed, and you want them to model what you taught them in their classrooms.

Lesson Design

Even in coaching, good lesson design can be helpful. You must consider all engagement aspects when building professional learning workshops, webinars, or any other resource or course. As discussed earlier, the first step is clear expectations and structure. But it doesn't stop there. You want to make sure you create and utilize a variety of activities. Effective lesson design incorporates individual work, group work, discussions, and activities. This variety caters to those learning preferences, but it also models how good design looks for the classroom. It allows all participants to shine in their strengths, provides opportunities to collaborate, and pushes the boundaries of what is comfortable for those you are coaching.

Differentiation

Another huge aspect of strong lesson design is to consider differentiation. Every student in your class has different needs and abilities, as will those you coach. You might have to offer tiered activities, provide different formats, and incorporate choice. Remember the UDL principles you learned in chapter four as you create lessons and activities while coaching.

You must also be flexible to shift in the moment if your participants are distracted by their social or content anxieties. For example, if you are working with your group on adding play to math class and using math that is too complex for some participants, they may stop trying. But, if you offer them a choice in the content to learn the strategy, they will be more engaged in the activity and learn more from the exploration because they feel they are in a safe space, which is the final aspect to consider in a well-designed lesson.

It is important to foster an environment that allows for failure and mistakes. Think about when you are learning a new game. You expect to have questions and need redirection, and you might even expect failure. But you are willing to listen and learn because, as a game, it's low stakes. We want to capture that in all learning environments where we can alleviate anxiety and encourage interaction. Focusing on the process and not the final product will foster a more inclusive learning environment that benefits everyone.

 **Data**

Let's take a moment and discuss data in a feedback loop. When your participants self-report by filling out a survey, they may not be accurate in their engagement levels. They may be hesitant to admit that they felt disengaged because of fear, or they like you and don't want to upset you. They may also overestimate their engagement for various reasons.

The next aspect to consider is how much data is collected. If it is only survey results, then your data might be biased or incomplete. You want more than one data point to understand levels of engagement. You want observation data, survey feedback, and a way to measure achievement. This information will give a clearer, more comprehensive view of how engaged everyone was.

Any time data is collected, you have to think about the variables. There may be factors outside of your control that lead to participants' satisfaction or their concerns around engagement. This can be those social factors we reviewed earlier or their general comfort level around the content. Our data can also fluctuate depending on the time of day. If you explore the work of Daniel Pink in his book "When: The Scientific Secrets of Perfect Timing," he highlights how, at specific parts of the day, we are more apt to get work done and need a lot of breaks. Knowing our human instincts and behaviors will help you find that balance between what the data says and what it tells you. You also have to consider the bias that each of us has based on the expectations of the coaching or PD session and how these perceptions can influence your participants' engagement and their reflection of engagement.

The best way to overcome these data shortfalls is to know that the more specific and actionable the feedback is, the better you can use the results to improve. Focus on solutions instead of roadblocks. If you are consistently told that your training is too fast or gives too much, consider breaking your PD into smaller chunks. If your feedback showcases confusion, find ways to bring clarity.

Finally, remember that the input reflects not on you but on participants' interpretation of how the training went. Don't take it to heart. You are often going to get feedback that feels like a personal attack. It's not. Instead, take it as a way to model growth. Use it to improve your task, and know we are all works in progress. As long as you are willing to accept and use that feedback to adjust and move forward, you can work on strategies that will help you keep your learners engaged.

Death by Icebreakers

As mentioned, be careful when considering the activities to engage your teachers in. Teachers are busy, and these icebreakers are often done on the first day after a break as part of a Superintendent's Day or Opening Day activity. While they may be fun and get people moving, they can also play into our anxieties and frustrations. Knowing how much is on the teacher's proverbial plate, use them sparingly and with meaning. Teachers don't want to play getting-to-know-you bingo or "two truths and a lie" if they have done it a dozen times before. Add new twists to a familiar activity, or connect it to the topics they care about.

For example, let's take a look at the party favorite, "two truths and a lie."

We have all played it. It can offer a ton of insight about people and help you learn fun facts about one another, leading to stronger bonds and relationships. But if a teacher has played the game repeatedly, it loses its luster. Think about the goal you are looking to achieve: Are you trying to create a community or thinking about fostering collaboration? Then, offer ways to use the simple activity in their classrooms.

Critical Thinking

After playing the "two truths and a lie" game, ask follow-up questions that challenge assumptions or uncover hidden truths. Ask participants to explain why they chose a particular statement as a lie or as truth. Encourage them to justify their reasoning.

Collaboration

Allow for an open dialogue so that participants can share their thoughts. Use this time to reach a consensus on the most effective lie statements and why they were convincing. Participants will learn from each other and gain new perspectives based on their answers.

Thought-Provoking

Share stories around the truths participants mentioned, and discuss how the events shaped who they are. Explore deeper thoughts.

Opening and Closing
Routines That Will
Supercharge Your
Classroom
Modern Classrooms

Culture Building

Finally, make the subjects topical instead of open-ended, and adjust complexity based on your audience. It's also important to be mindful of cultural differences and avoid "hot" topics that could be offensive or misunderstood.

The idea here is that whatever you choose to do around icebreakers, as in our "two truths and a lie" iterations example above, tie them into something more meaningful that can truly meet the goals. Explore icebreakers backed by research, such as ones from Modern Classrooms or Digital Promise, to ensure they are worthwhile. You can view these examples by scanning the QR codes.

Design
Digital Promise

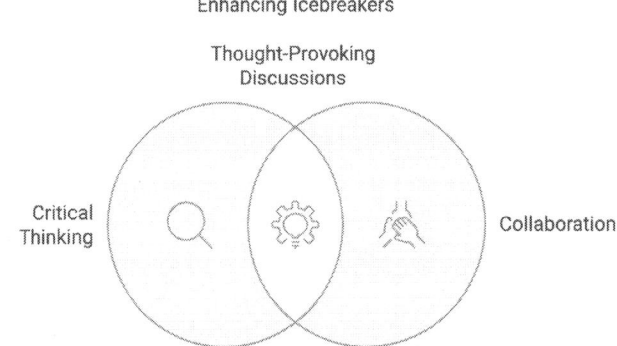

There are tons of ways to bring a little fun to your meetings. Scan this QR code for some great ideas and links to amazing resources to spark an idea.

Unleash Inventive and
Creative
Collaborations
Laurie Guyon

Now let's have a little fun. We asked Gemini to create a coaching game for one. Here's the activity; give it a try!

We are going to create our own Coach Quest Activity. Take out a piece of paper and fold it into four equal parts. Here is what you will do next:

1. Unfold the paper, and in the center where the folds meet, write down one challenge you would like to overcome when coaching, teaching, or training. This can be disengagement, access, time, etc. Use what you know.
2. On the top left, write down a tech tool or strategy you like to use that might help with your challenge.
3. On the top right, write down ways to incorporate collaboration into the mix. Maybe it's pairing a teacher with another who excels or telling a story about a student to help make the learning authentic.
4. On the bottom left, determine how you will measure success in overcoming the challenge.
5. On the bottom right, consider how you will introduce and implement the tool and the collaboration to allow for success.
6. OK, now for the fun: Fold one of the corners into the center of your paper to hide the text, and consider how to solve the challenge with only the info from the other three sections. Keep changing the corners you hide to get those creative juices flowing.
7. On the back of the paper, add your thoughts about how you will implement your coaching plan.

Now, this is more of a fun brainstorming activity for one, but you can switch this up to fit any group you are with. Add in drawings, pivots, and other storytelling elements as you construct your game to make it more creative. You can even give it a fun name, like Allies and Conquerors, for instance. If this seems too overwhelming to think of on your own, use AI and ask it to create the game for you.

Make sure in your prompt that you are clear about the learning objectives, the materials you can access, and the time you want to spend on it. If you keep it general, you will get a generic response, so include as much detail as possible for the best result.

Another strategy is to grab eight sticky notes and give yourself only 40 seconds to jot down a solution for each problem. Write anything, even if you think it's bad. Then, once all eight sticky notes are filled, rank them, discuss them, modify them, or whatever it is, you need to determine the best way forward.

Simple Tools with Large Rewards

While the focus will be training on the topic, remember that all your participants are there for various reasons. For this reason, it's good to start all training with a game or activity to engage and excite the participants. This is also a great time to get to know who is in the room; simple getting-to-know-you activities can be helpful. For large groups, you can create table topics to get things moving. One of the most effective ways to do this is to take the participants out of their comfort zones. You can use any ideas from the link shared at the beginning of this chapter or create your own. But, just for fun, let's explore some tried-and-true tools.

LEGO

LEGO is a great way to bring groups together. We use them often in workshops to get our audience engaged. As soon as your participants arrive and see the colorful bricks, they will start to play with them. You can set out a baggie of bricks, bring containers with the bricks inside, or just pile the bricks on the table; do what works best for you. One fun way to get things started is to ask participants to design something. The point is not to give them much regarding rules and not show an "exemplar" or an example.

You might ask them to build a game, a character, or a tool—really, anything you want. From there, you can have the participants share their creations and discuss ways to use simple activities like this with students. This is guaranteed to be a favorite activity in your workshops. Imagine the variety of simple games you and those in your PD can create with just these simple bricks. Make sure to collect their ideas somewhere digital, such as a Google Keep note or a Wakelet Collection, so they have a resource to return to. You will be amazed at the creativity!

Use What You Have

With AI at our fingertips, you can create games and activities instantly. Taking these activities offline will help all learners feel more comfortable participating, allow for more discussion, and keep the focus on each other (watch all of the smiles and eye contact!). One fun way to do this is to do an activity that uses only what they brought. I've seen water bottle towers, grid games, sticky-note creativity, and more.

You will be surprised what people can come up with if given the opportunity. This is also a great way for you to learn about the people in the room and for them to realize that your training is not a sit-and-get but rather a highly engaging session with many ideas and takeaways.

Thinking Games

When you consider UDL as outlined earlier in the book, you will see that you must offer opportunities for the why, the what, and the how. A great way to get your participants thinking is to allow them to try out whatever you are training on. But you can do this in an enjoyable way. Instead of walking them through a step-by-step tutorial, give them challenges. Make it a scavenger hunt, a bingo game, a turn and talk, or whatever it takes for them to get a chance to try out a new tool or idea. From there, let them discuss and try something out without you interfering.

Finally, bring it back together to debrief. Think of it as the reverse of I do, we do, you do. Reversing your typical lesson can help build confidence and build a community that supports each other. Watch for frustration levels. You don't want your participants to get frustrated or shut down because they think that learning the tool is too hard. Keep the debrief short and offer support. Then, make sure you go over the steps as a review before you move on. Pause for questions and encourage their thinking. You will find this strategy to work well when trying to teach new concepts or ideas.

OK Go on YouTube

Just for Fun

While playing games or doing activities can teach content, having a little fun can be just as important. These moments should be short as you will have much to cover in your training, but they can help reset the group, build a community, and give their brains a break. You can use breathing techniques, show short 1- or 2-minute videos, or play a game you love. Use fun activities to transition if you are switching to a new topic.

After every 20 minutes or so, you can throw in a fun 1-minute stretch. At longer breaks, offer a fun brainteaser to get participants thinking while they regroup. Use rebus puzzles, math puzzles, riddles, or anything available to keep things moving. For transitions, listen to a popular song or check out the videos from OK Go on YouTube (scan QR code), which are always fan favorites.

Motivating

If your teachers need motivation, grab a motivational video. These can be used during breaks or as a way to reinvigorate teachers to persevere if the content is tough. You can also use Pixar Shorts to inspire and motivate your audience. Remember that you want to model what you want them to do in the classroom. No one comes to PD to sit and listen for hours as a presenter drones on. Keep them moving, keep them talking, and get them having fun. They will keep coming back for more!

Remember that, for the most part, "icebreakers," as they're often called, can feel like a waste of time to your participants. Use games and activities in meaningful ways. Allow teachers to see ways to use the same little moments in their classrooms to build relationships, work on social-emotional needs, or just have a little fun. You want to make sure what you create is inclusive, heartwarming, entertaining, or whatever your goal is. If you start to see teachers leaving your training, checking their email, or disengaging with you in other ways, you have missed the mark and need to redirect. You want your participants leaning into the learning, not looking for a way to escape it.

Observing the Fun and Considering Engagement

A huge part of coaching is spending time in classrooms. This classroom time will give you stories and experiences to draw from when helping others, and it will help you stay current on understanding what happens in the school.

 **Laurie**

Recently, I was exploring a new tool called Mirror from Swivl, a device that uses AI to help students reflect on their learning. It uses the CASEL framework, a

CASEL.org

comprehensive approach to SEL that prioritizes the development of students' social and emotional skills alongside their academic abilities the tool offers positive and critical feedback to the students based on their ability to reflect on their learning (scan the QR code to learn more). I asked students two questions about their knowledge of artificial intelligence and digital citizenship in this environment and then videoed the students explaining their thoughts and understanding of the topics.

One of the questions asked of the students was to tell us one thing they wished adults knew about how the students use AI and kids' online presence. Students were aware they were being recorded on the device and could see themselves on screen when they were recording. The students visited five different stations during their time with me. This was one station to visit during their rotation, and since not all students were comfortable recording themselves, it was optional (UDL!).

The attitudes of the students who chose to do this activity varied. Some gave strong opinions and quality feedback, while others used it as if they were recording a video for TikTok. Many of the boys used it to say their favorite saying in 2024: Skibidi Toilet. (If you are unfamiliar with the term, spend a day in a middle school classroom, and you will find out everything there is to know about it. It's a silly video on YouTube that boys find funny, and "Skibidi" is now used as slang to mean "bad.")

Using the Mirror offered insight into all of the students. For those who took the activity seriously, it provided positive reinforcement of specific SEL skills and pushed their thinking in areas identified for growth. Those who were silly got positive reinforcement, too, but they were offered reasons why they should take time to reflect more seriously.

I observed how these students interacted with the device and used it for future classroom activities. The students needed help with their digital citizenship skills, understanding that videos like the ones they made are permanent and that they need to protect their PII or personal identifiable information, such as their full name and where they are located.

In addition to being a fun activity, it led to some rich discussions. This is what you are looking for when you spend time in classrooms. As a coach, your time is often limited, so gathering this type of feedback can be transformational for you as you consider what you should do in the classroom, and it will help you coach the teachers based on student needs.

Spending time in classrooms is one of the perks of being a coach. You will find that students love the mix-up in their routine caused by having a "guest speaker," and you are not bound by the constraints of standards. Use these moments to model what learning can look like. Use the UDL model, get the students moving, and have fun!

The last part to consider is community building. When you spend time on the fun, you are working on building strong relationships. Just as you want teachers to come to your PD, you want kids to have fun in the classroom. You want teachers to welcome you into their classrooms, too. Offering ideas and resources and modeling these activities will foster those connections. This is your time to shine!

Chapter 10

Educator Support
~ Establishing a Neighborhood Watch ~

"Definition of good neighbor: someone to be trusted; a courteous, friendly source of help when help is needed; someone you can count on; someone who cares."

—Edward B. Rust, Jr. (former CEO of State Farm Insurance)

One aspect of education that has always fascinated us is how siloed we are. Despite having team planning times scheduled on our calendars, faculty meetings that bring everyone together for updates, and moments where we share casual stuff about our lives in the hallway during duty or faculty lunchrooms, we still work in isolation. OK, aside from the children's classroom, many of us work solo with colleagues.

Once in our classrooms, WE are the superintendent, the principal, and the teacher in our domain. Some of us may even close the doors to the possibilities of instructional rounds, team-teaching, or coaching. For two reasons, it is essential to think about and reflect on how you were/are as a teacher.

1. It will help ground you when making your way into teachers' classrooms, and 2. It will give you a good foundation for a goal you must strive for in terms of building relationships in and out of your school.

When you step into the world of educational technology coaching, please take a moment to reflect on how you were as an educator. For instance:

- Was your door open or closed?
- How was your classroom furniture arranged? Was it in rows or set up like a Socratic seminar with chairs in a circle for open discussions?
- Were you involved in any planning committees, events, or special projects outside your duties and responsibilities?
- Outside of the comfort of your school, did you connect professionally with others around the globe?

We are not saying that if you did not check off every box, you should give up your career and aspirations of being an educational technology coach; not at all. This is sometimes one aspect of coaching severely overlooked as an avenue for professional growth and so much opportunity.

Building relationships in and outside of your school is an art. And for some, scary. Please hear us when we say this: Relationships come first; everything else is secondary. Everything.

Rita Pierson gave a powerful TED Talk in 2013 titled "Every Kid Needs a Champion." In it she discusses the importance of relationships, exclaiming, "Kids don't learn from people they don't like." Think about that for a moment. Think about when you were a student and who your favorite teachers were. Have you ever had a year where your favorite subject area in school was tainted because the adult responsible for teaching you wasn't your favorite? Now, replace the word "kids" with "humans": Humans don't learn from people they don't like.

Although much of what was said in that TED Talk was about building positive relationships with students in the classroom (scan QR code for a link to Rita's TED Talk), Rita's words could also be the golden rule for coaching:

Every Kid Needs a Champion

Rita Pierson
TED

"Every child deserves a champion—an adult who will never give up on them, who understands the power of connection and insists that they become the best they can be."
—Rita Pierson

This quote rings true for coaching, too. See, building relationships goes beyond a popularity contest. It helps start the foundation for more extraordinary things to come. Building relationships takes time. Before you feel established as an educational technology coach, it may take two or three years (or even longer, depending on variables such as whether you are there full time, how many buildings are in your district, etc.) But what we can learn from Rita is that relationships are essential for trust, perseverance, and guidance, regardless of whether you are a child or an adult.

Your professional learning network is equally important for building your outer circle. While we understand that reaching out and making digital connections can be intimidating to some, your professional learning network is equally important for building your outer circle.

Imagine a professional learning network (PLN) as a vibrant ecosystem where you can interact with other coaches, learning and growing together. Being part of such a network gives you access to a toolbox of resources and ideas that can significantly enhance your coaching practices. It is a fantastic place to collaborate with peers, share experiences, and receive valuable feedback, which can encourage a sense of community and support.

Best of all, a PLN allows you to stay current on the latest trends and advancements in educational technology, ensuring that your coaching strategies remain relevant and effective. You can engage in continuous learning opportunities, such as webinars, workshops, and online courses, honing your skills and expanding your knowledge base.

Moreover, a PLN empowers you to build professional relationships, showcase your expertise, and establish a strong reputation within the educational technology community. This recognition may open new opportunities, such as speaking engagements, leadership roles, and career advancement. By joining a PLN, you can elevate your coaching game and advance your career.

Building your PLN can take many forms and opportunities. Later in this chapter, we will help you focus on building the inner and outer relationships essential to coaching.

The Importance of a PLN

We all live within different communities, including our school community, towns and cities, and online connections. Communities are groups of people who share common interests, may share goals or characteristics, and can foster a sense of belonging. A community might be where you turn for support. These groups can be based on location, shared passions, professions, and hobbies. Since a community framework allows for social connections, it offers a chance to share ideas and resources. This network of relationships can be built on communication, shared experiences, and objectives. Being part of the right communities can enrich your life—or, in this case, your professional life.

This chapter will explore your professional learning network (PLN). Some may use the phrase "professional learning community" (PLC) or change that last word to "family" for a PLF. Whatever you call it, it can be a robust community. A PLN can consist of people in the same profession subject matter or with common interests, and a good PLN offers support.

A great PLN becomes part of a community you often look forward to connecting with and rely on. Before we dive in, take a moment and jot down the groups you currently belong to. These don't all have to do with educational coaching. Instead, write down your circles. This includes friends, colleagues, hobby groups, sports teams, and online communities. The idea is to see where you interact and who you choose to interact with. If you are not on social media, that is OK! Many ways exist to connect with a PLN without diving into X or Facebook.

The most important aspects of a social PLN are the ones that keep you learning and support your journey. Regarding coaching, a good PLN will connect you with experts in the field, offer mentoring opportunities, and give you opportunities to collaborate. This can lead to career advancement or opportunities to share your story (like writing a book!). These networks should be a platform to share your work, gather feedback, and gain recognition.

But it is so much more than this simple give-and-take. A good PLN can transcend boundaries. The authors of this book met because of a PLN. It brought us together because of our job titles, and then, once we met, our connection blossomed into a friendship that led to collaborating on workshops, webinars, conferences, and this book. Since we met, we have joined other PLNs that have enriched our experiences and kept us in touch even though we live in different parts of New York.

While we have enjoyed the opportunities, we have also leaned on each other during difficult times and often talked to get feedback and support in our daily lives. Only some people within a PLN will become this close, but you never know what will blossom if you are not part of several PLNs. Unlike a professional learning workshop with a set structure, a PLN can tailor your learning based on your preferred interests and pace. You can choose which PLNs you want to join and how much you want to participate. Another benefit of a PLN is that you can choose not to participate, or you can mute the application when you feel overwhelmed, need a break, or even want to dive further into something before moving on. This can lead to a more engaging and practical learning experience.

Another aspect to consider that comes with being a part of a PLN is allowing peer learning and collaboration. Within your PLN, someone might ask for help with a project or an idea they want to explore. You are always welcome to raise your hand and participate—or decline—based on how busy you are, your interest in the topic, and your experiences. However, peer learning can offer more opportunities, knowledge, and new experiences beyond any PD you participate in; the ability to work within your PLN collaboratively is often more relatable and applicable to your daily professional life.

Professional learning networks are crucial to your professional learning, especially regarding coaching. The right PLN equips you with the connections, the resources, and the essential tools needed to support others within your work. Your PLN can empower you to adapt to the ever-changing educational technology landscape and pedagogical strategies. It can help you stay on top of educational trends, learn the latest research, and participate in opportunities that encourage connection and growth.

Breaking Down the Silos

You probably have heard the term "silos" in education. For example, think about your high school. Students go from English to math to science, and so on. In traditional schools, these subjects are taught in isolation. But, when you enter the so-called "real world," things are not so segmented. This is not to say that if you teach social studies, you shouldn't join a PLN that teaches the same subject. We encourage you to do so!

We are saying there is a benefit of looking outside your lens for opportunities. If you stay within your discipline, you may isolate yourself from other groups, limiting your communication and collaboration in other areas. If you have specific goals that you want to achieve, a PLN outside of your norm may hold the answers.

There are many different silos in educational settings. Let's take a few moments to explore some of the big ones and consider how to break them down to make them more diverse and inclusive.

 **Aimee**

When I held the position of a Technology Integration Specialist in a BOCES within New York State, I had the unique privilege of overseeing the arts and music forum

for our region. Recognizing the isolation many art teachers often experience, I sought to break down silos and create a culture of collaboration.

To achieve this, I established an "instructional rounds PLN," where groups of six art teachers from diverse rural schools would visit one another's classrooms. These visits provided opportunities for authentic learning and sharing. Teachers could observe different classroom setups, teaching styles, and student engagement levels. By seeing how colleagues approached art education at various grade levels, teachers gained valuable insights and could adapt their practices.

One memorable visit to a middle school led to a humorous misunderstanding: a student remarked, "Wow, there are a lot of substitute teachers here today!" This lighthearted moment underscored the importance of such visits in fostering a sense of community and shared experiences.

Unfortunately, the pandemic abruptly halted our instructional rounds, preventing us from carrying out this endeavor in future school years, and I never had the opportunity to revisit it. However, the positive impact of these collaborations was undeniable.

Structural Segregation

These are those natural breaks that divide us by departments. For instance, how often do the English and social studies departments meet? Do science and art ever talk? Traditionally, the answer is no, but if we consider the opportunities that exist if we were to meet, we would see that these meetings can be mutually beneficial.

For example, let's say you teach sixth-grade English. You meet with your grade-level team and learn that the Social Studies teachers cover Ancient Greece. It would be fantastic if the two departments worked together to read books about Greek mythology, collaborate on projects that encourage deeper learning of the content, and open up opportunities to "fit more in" because you are spreading the work between two departments. The experiences can be more project-based, allowing for more inquiry and creativity.

While coaching, this separation of two subjects often happens. You will have the opportunity to work with all sorts of departments and have a thumb on the content happening in their classrooms, bringing the departments together. At the same time, coaching can create new PLNs that are less structured and segregated. Coaching can open up interdisciplinary opportunities and help teachers create shared spaces in their classrooms, a library, or a large group or training area, allowing students more freedom to work together. Further, it can open up opportunities for new initiatives, such as participating in a global event or engaging in a civics or service organization, bringing the outside community into your classroom.

By breaking down these silos, we will enhance the student experience. Students will benefit from this more holistic learning through complex real-world applications that require interdisciplinary solutions. Coaching will allow for more innovation because of the diversity in expertise. One of the most significant benefits of breaking down silos is building a stronger school community, which can lead to a vibrant and collaborative school culture.

Cultural Boundaries

Different groups may develop unique cultures or norms that are difficult to break into for other groups. Think of the cliques you have in middle school: jocks hang out with jocks, theater kids stick together, and so on. Be careful that your groups are not creating invisible lines based on their culture, behaviors, and norms. This can lead to a misalignment of the school's mission and vision.

Communication is critical to building any group, but as you explore PLNs, be mindful of how the groups communicate and interact. These boundaries can lead to change resistance and may rely more on the adage "That's how we always did it." This can be highly detrimental to any PLN's success, especially as a coach trying to support new initiatives. These boundaries can unintentionally isolate people, leading to anger and frustration across your PLN. Most importantly, culturally solid boundaries can lead to unconscious bias where certain groups may be privileged over others, leading to inequities in resources, opportunities, and even recognition.

In educational settings, it is vital to have open dialogue about cultural boundaries. It's one thing to say "that group" or the "boys club" or whatever terms you hear in the halls. But suppose you want to foster a truly inclusive culture that values diversity and understanding. In that case, you must be aware of this and offer ways to recognize it for others. This comes down to training, creating mixed communities, and even having policies encouraging collaboration.

Communication Gaps

Have you ever worked for someone you only hear from when there is a problem? Or someone who emails 20 times a day with increasingly more confusing emails? If so, then you know the frustration of ineffective communication, which can stem from either technological limitations or a lack of technical skills. It can come from how your organization is structured and can happen because of physical separation. Physical separations can be geographic, architectural, or even departmental, creating limits on interactions where it's often necessary to rely instead on formal and less frequent communication channels.

When communication fails, it can have negative impacts within a PLN. This can include a delay in decision-making, less collaboration, inconsistencies in policies and practices, and the loss of opportunities for innovation. Moreover, it can lead to frustration and anxiety among its members. If you want to unlock the full potential of a robust PLN you belong to or run, consider how to address these common communication issues to ensure better success.

The Lone Nut. Aimee.

How to Start a Movement TED

Before we continue, I'd like you to stop everything you're doing and scan the QR code to watch this TED Talk video about "The Lone Nut." Even though I don't usually advocate for homework, watching this video is worthwhile. Don't worry. We'll still be here when you get back.

What's so powerful about that short clip? It shows that one courageous person can create a ripple effect on followers. Let's consider this in two ways. First, if you're hesitant to reach out and find supporters in your professional learning community, be that lone nut. Stay true to your authentic self and have the courage to speak your mind.

Second, when coaching and connecting with teachers, find that "lone nut" teacher —the outcast. Why? Because, at some point, you were also that lone nut. Others will join in once you find someone willing to work with you; have the courage to be that lone nut.

Communication and Collaboration Techniques

You have invested a significant amount of time in building your PLN. You conduct excellent workshops and have connected with people in your building and beyond!

Now that you have laid the foundation for developing relationships, how can you maintain them? How can you establish a good rapport with someone you have just begun to coach or will be working on with a series of workshops? What are some ways you can increase collaboration and communication? Also, how can you further develop connections to work with the individuals in your group, workshop, and PLN while coaching? Let's look at the protocols that could be set in place, along with some tried and true methods that we can share.

Remember, in your role, it is essential to establish open and honest communication. This involves active listening, giving full attention to the speaker, and avoiding interruption. As we learned in the design thinking model, empathy is valuable in this role. Showing your understanding and compassion for another person's perspective, especially if they are afraid to utilize technology in their classroom, will help you go the extra mile.

Be honest and transparent; be upfront about your intentions and expectations.

You would want this from a leader and are often seen as one in this role. Also, remember that in this role, you should always be respectful and professional and that confidentiality is crucial as you build relationships.

Norms!

We're not talking about Norm, the character from the 80s sitcom "Cheers" who was greeted with a chorus of "Norm!" every time he walked into his neighborhood bar. We are talking about the norms of communication and collaboration. Norms are essential for effective communication and collaboration within a team. Since collaboration is a crucial part of successful teamwork, establishing explicit norms or expectations is necessary for creating a productive and harmonious environment.

These norms develop guidelines for how team members interact, communicate, and contribute. You can choose to go it alone and have the individuals you are working with cocreate norms based on the group's needs, or you can seek resources such as those from The Adaptive School (scan the QR code for details).

Thinking Collaborative
The Adaptive Schools
Norms

Understanding Yourself and Others

Using personality quizzes to build relationships and improve team dynamics is effective. Unlike overused icebreakers, the strategic use of activities like personality quizzes allows team members to engage in a way that increases collaboration and enhances understanding. Tests such as CliftonStrengths, the DiSC Personality Test, and 16 Personalities are among the most popular. When used with intention, they become a valuable asset to not only those learning about themselves but also those learning about their teammates.

 **Aimee**

One of my favorite personality quizzes is Compass Points. Like the Myers-Briggs Type Indicator (MBTI) quiz, it focuses on how a team functions.

Melanie Kitchen (@MelKitchenEDU), a fellow technology integrator, introduced me to this protocol at a regional professional development session called Tech Integrators Forum. Although we ran out of time to thoroughly review it, I was hooked. Since then, I have completed the protocol virtually and in person with teams I have worked with. I have also assisted in carrying it out at various schools.

Recently, I have used this protocol in my role as the supervisor of instructional technology with my instructional technology coaches alongside my fellow peer supervisors and their team members. What I find intriguing about Compass Points is the way it focuses on how teams work and interact with one another. As with any personality quiz, you assess yourself based on your professional strengths. Once you determine your "compass point" (North, South, East, or West, and sometimes people are more than one point), you form groups based on your compass point. Each group will receive a set of questions to think about and answer together. For example: What are some of the strengths of your compass point? What are the limitations of your style? What compass point might you find challenging to work with?

From there, the groups share and reflect on their findings. A few laughs are typically enjoyed as the North group calls out the South group for being too wishy-washy. I love this protocol because it sets a foundation for working effectively and efficiently as a team. We all bring value-added skills to the table; we need to learn how to place the right people in the right part of a project. It's important that we understand individual learning and working styles and hone in on their strengths. This prevents us from putting people into situations that, because of genetic makeup, personality, or working style, set them up for automatic failure.

Compass Point
Activity Adapted from
Center for
Collaborative
Education

I have adapted the Compass Point Protocol into a virtual quiz and presentation. You can scan the QR code to use it with your teams. I honestly can't say enough about this protocol.

All in all, when you're working to promote a culture of collaboration, communication, and curiosity, you need to build in time and create space for authentic conversation. In education, we often over-plan and fill every moment, neglecting the power of unplanned conversations. Embrace these moments of genuine connection; they offer invaluable insights and experiences.

Finding and Joining PLNs

How to find a PLN
1. Turn on your phone.
2. Make sure you are connected to a network.
3. Open up a social media app like X.
4. Say something really bold, like you would yell in the first grade to random kids riding their bikes down the street, such as "Will you be my friend?"
5. Repeat.

We have discussed the importance of PLNs, and you will be ready to embrace connecting with other educators. You may already belong to some groups depending on your content, grade level, or interests. Thinking about what you are looking to learn or share is important, as PLNs come in all shapes and sizes. It's up to us to determine which ones to join. Ensure that what you join lifts you up and is not a time or task drain. If it asks too much of you, step back. You are not joining PLNs to make more work for yourself! You are considering being a part of a PLN because it fills a need, whether socially, emotionally, or academically.

Where You Can Find PLNs

 ## Social Media

Many people avoid social media for a variety of reasons. Social media can be a dark place that can drain and frustrate you. But, if leveraged correctly, it can be an incredible space to connect with other educators. It's where ideas and resources are shared, and it's a place where educators like you can find support. It can also be a place to celebrate small wins and get help when needed. You can choose the

the best platform for you, whether it's Facebook, X, TikTok, Blue Sky, or Instagram—although it doesn't have to be any of these. There are tons of other platforms where you can find your people.

Laurie's story

When I first fell in love with technology in the classroom, I didn't know where to learn more. I was fortunate enough to attend a literacy conference, which included a session on using social media. I signed up for Twitter (X) and immediately followed about a hundred people by exploring hashtags around education. From there, I started posting some of my activities and found more people to follow.

I learned about nonprofits and other education organizations that offered training and opportunities. I went to book studies and participated in Twitter chats. I learned so much from following people on social media. I joined Facebook groups and was invited to join a local group of other EdTech women doing jobs similar to mine. I made many friends and built many relationships that I still have because I put myself out there. Social media is not for everyone, so find where you can connect based on your comfort zone. But also push yourself a bit outside of your comfort zone to expand your thinking.

Finding PLNs When You Least Expect It: Going to Conferences

Both of us, Laurie and Aimee, have spent many days traveling and attending conferences in our home state of New York and beyond. We both enjoy different aspects of conferences. It's a time when we can be together with other like-minded educators who give us new ideas. It's also a time for us to unwind, share a laugh, and get fresh perspectives. Going to conferences is often the best way to reengage and remember our "why" around what made us become educators.

~ Our Story ~

Laurie's Version

Aimee and I have known each other for many years, but our friendship started at a conference. We had been in the same statewide group from our BOCES in New York and had met on many occasions, but it was when we both ended up at the FETC conference in Miami that we shifted from being colleagues to becoming friends. On the last day of the conference, we bumped into each other in the hallway and asked each other where we were headed next. I mentioned that I would walk the vendor floor, and Aimee agreed to go with me.

What Aimee didn't know was that I would talk to everyone. Yes, everyone. Every vendor that we passed was greeted, and a conversation was started. I asked a lot of questions and showed interest even if the product wasn't something I could use. I love getting swag, and I took everything that was offered: pens, stickers, water bottles, bottle openers, T-shirts—you name it. This meant Aimee got a lot of swag, too. By the end, when we left the vendor floor, it was time for Aimee to get to the airport to fly home. Aimee's bags were overflowing with swag; she had so much stuff she almost needed another bag!

That time spent together on the vendor floor gave us ideas and new tools to bring back to our districts, but it also gave us contacts that we could reach out to and swag to give away at our PD sessions. As a coach, it's important to know what is new and what is changing in the products we use. However, what really matters is the relationships you develop with these vendors—they can be game changers. Part of building your PLN is building relationships with others in the same roles, but building your PLN also means having people you can contact to ask for help. These vendor contacts can lead to demos, free trials, and, of course, swag. But it is so much more than that. Having vendors as part of your PLN can also offer opportunities you hadn't thought about as a coach.

📖 Aimee's Version

While I cannot argue or discount any of Laurie's stories, I would like to add two important points. First, despite attending numerous conferences and engaging in countless sessions, the most valuable professional development comes from learning from your peers. Surround yourself with individuals who complement your strengths and weaknesses. Don't be intimidated or second-guess yourself; doing so will not contribute to your professional and personal growth.

Second, when meeting and connecting with new members of your PLN who may or may not become friends, it's important to remember something: If that person loves to visit vendor floors at conferences, be aware that you might face issues at airport security. I had to explain a lot and leave some items behind due to my experience with Laurie that day, but I wouldn't change it for anything in the world.

Attending conferences and exploring vendor floors offers a wealth of insights and innovative ideas to discover. As you participate in sessions and walk through the aisles of booths, take the time to interact with various exhibitors and educators. Remember to exchange contact information during these interactions, as each one has the potential to spark new perspectives and inspire ideas that could significantly influence your future. You might even meet a lifelong friend like Laurie.

Laurie's Example

A teacher told me she was looking for a solution for a new student who didn't speak English. She wanted something to help translate work and allow the student to communicate. She had used Google Translate but wanted something else. Because I had chatted with a vendor at a conference about a Scanmarker, and they had offered me a free trial pen to keep for a month, I thought I had a solution that could help. I called the vendor after I had spoken with the teacher, and they extended the trial to another month. The teacher loved the tool, and her district purchased extras for other students in the district.

Because I had taken the time to have that discussion, we were able to fill a need. From that point on, I have worked with the vendor, who has provided at least a dozen trials, and because of the vendor's outstanding service and response, many of my districts have bought these pens to help students in all grades who speak various languages other than English.

If you ever see me at a conference, you will often find me on the vendor floor, watching demos, asking questions, and finding updates. It's something I look forward to at every conference. I take the time to talk not only to the vendors but also to the other educators there. I ask them what they teach and what they found on the vendor floor or at the conference that they can't wait to implement or bring back to their classrooms. I learn so much from others and find wandering the expo hall the most valuable part.

If you can attend a conference, connect with those around you. You never know what could come of that meeting. Both of us, Aimee and Laurie, have collaborated, copresented, been on podcasts, and built resources and activities because we spent time together at conferences. Now when we attend conferences, we will also share a meal or a drink to unwind and get to know each other better. Many members of your PLN will become your friends, your confidants, and the people who make you smile.

Strategies Including Starting PLNs

While conferences are a fabulous way to start and build a PLN, they are only sometimes an option. Many districts don't have the funds or may not find the value in you attending one. Most often, your PLN may start with the people you work with. The teacher across the hall or your work team could become your strongest PLN. But don't limit yourself to just those around you. You may have to look outside your inner circle to see other perspectives and share fresh ideas. If you *can* attend a conference, look for one within your state first.

NYSCATE (The New York State Association for Computers and Technologies in Education) hosts an annual conference in the United States during the week leading up to Thanksgiving. This conference always brings together EdTech coaches, tech directors, library media specialists, TOSAs (teachers on special assignment), and classroom teachers and administrators. Over four days, there are multiple sessions, keynotes, poster sessions, and mini opportunities to connect and chat with others. We both attend NYSCATE every year.

There's always a common area to sit and talk and plenty of evening events to keep attendees connected and recharging. This event has a considerable vendor floor and tons of opportunities just to sit and share a cup of coffee and a conversation. The more years you go, the more connections you will make. This event feels a lot like a family reunion as you see your PLN gather each year to share.

Within NYSCATE, there are opportunities throughout the year to connect, learn, and engage with other members. One such opportunity is a certified coaching program that is co-facilitated by your authors. Within this group, we meet virtually, share resources, and learn about topics you are reading about in this book. It is a place for us to share our wins and strategies and get help from each other, and a great way to build a PLN with like-minded people doing the work.

Even if you cannot attend a conference or join the coaching program, the organization has a lot to offer virtually. There are probably similar organizations within your state or area of the world. For example, ISTE has a community leader group you can apply to. It also hosts book studies and offers podcasts, newsletters, and more to help people connect with others. There's even an ISTE Connect site that offers opportunities for attendees to ask questions and learn from one another. If you don't belong to any groups, look at the organizations for your content area and your interests to see what they offer.

If conferences are not an option, you can still use conference landing pages to gain information and connect with others. Once keynotes and spotlight speakers are announced, you can look up these educators' profiles on social media or find their websites. You will find resources and opportunities to join webinars or training sessions on these websites. These speakers may offer mini free conferences online or open forums that you can engage in. Each educator uses their platform differently, so if one doesn't fit for you, try others. For the EdTech world, there are a ton of great bloggers, speakers, and resource generators that we love to follow.

Then, turn to your local organizations and statewide affiliates for similar opportunities. For example, the BOCES (Board of Cooperative Educational Services) is in New York. It provides shared educational programs and services to school districts around the state. Within these BOCES are school support groups that offer training, resources, and cohorts that meet throughout the year.

These groups may be topic-centered, like STEM teachers or SEL advocates, or they may be more general. Look there first to see what opportunities are available. Your statewide groups, like NYSCATE in New York, offer professional learning opportunities, regional meetups, and possibly groups you can join and learn from. You may have regional teacher centers that offer PD as well. Each opportunity to meet with others is an opportunity to grow your PLN.

Ask your educator friends who they follow and to what groups and organizations they belong. Ask them what they find valuable and what they have learned from joining different groups. If you find a PLN that fills your bucket, stay with that group, but if it is frustrating you or stressing you out, you should step away. A PLN should be a positive experience that helps you grow. Remember your "why" when you think about staying or leaving a group.

Once you find your groups, think about how you want to be engaged with them. Remember that it should never be a burden and should take up little of your time. If you are overwhelmed by the emails, updates, etc., it might be time to leave the group. The group should always fill your bucket, not make it overflow. On the other hand, if it doesn't fill a need the way you would like, you can also walk away and find one that fits your needs.

The easiest way to start is to check with teacher organizations for volunteer opportunities. For example, ISTE (International Society for Technology in Education) has a volunteer page that offers anyone who is interested ways to connect. There's a place called Connect for anyone wanting to learn more about anything in education. Your state affiliates have volunteer opportunities at their regional conferences, and you can always contact your teacher centers or ask your colleagues what groups they belong to. Lastly, check your state or country's education departments for ways to connect and get involved.

Effective organization and time management are crucial for success as an educational technology coach. Maintaining a meticulously updated calendar is essential to avoid scheduling conflicts and maintain professionalism.

You Can Book Me

Calendly

Consider using a booking calendar in Google Calendar or Outlook (or through dedicated tools like YouCanBookMe and Calendly—scan the QR codes for more info) to streamline scheduling and ensure availability. This allows teachers to book appointments with you quickly.

When creating appointments, it's vital to include all necessary details, such as the purpose of the meeting, specific tasks, or required materials. This comprehensive approach is not just about filling in the blanks but about preparing effectively and providing tailored support to enhance the quality of your coaching. Please allow yourself time in between bookings; otherwise you won't have bathroom breaks, a chance to eat, or just time to breathe.

It's extremely important for us to emphasize the importance of keeping your calendar current. This is not just a task but a crucial responsibility for maintaining professionalism and preventing scheduling conflicts. You should update your calendar regularly and enhance your organizational skills as your schedule becomes more dynamic, especially in the role of an educational technology coach.

One helpful option, especially when managing multiple projects, is to use a digital task management tool such as Monday, Wrike, or Trello. These tools can assist you in effectively handling your tasks, projects, and deadlines. You can stay on top of your workload by creating boards or projects for different tasks, initiatives, or types of support and utilizing features like checklists, due dates, and notifications.

And don't forget to create lists! While the classic pen-and-paper method works fine, since we're discussing technology, let's explore some tech-based options. Google

Keep, Apple's Reminders app, and Microsoft To-Do are all fantastic tools for organizing your ongoing to-do list. Some of these apps even seamlessly sync your lists with your calendar!

Equally important is maintaining a digital resource library. Tools like Wakelet (scan QR code for more information) can gather and organize links to relevant websites, articles, and tutorials. You can categorize resources by subject, grade level, or technology tool.

Wakelet

Wakelet is a versatile tool I can't live without. It's incredibly user-friendly and has become indispensable in my professional and personal life.

Professionally, I use Wakelet to share resources during professional development sessions, facilitate collaborative discussions among participants, and finally, set and track personal and professional goals.

For personal goal setting, I create a Wakelet board outlining my annual objectives. This includes certifications, educational technology skills I want to acquire, and personal growth areas. I use the board to take notes, organize information, and reflect on my progress throughout the year.

Wakelet is a valuable tool for supporting others and driving personal development. My professional family regularly uses it to share what we have learned at various conferences; if you have not used it, check it out.

Using your calendar, another item you may want to schedule weekly, biweekly, or monthly is a consistent communication strategy. This includes newsletters, videos, and emails to teachers, administrators, and district staff. You may also want to schedule regular meetings or check-ins to discuss progress, challenges, and upcoming needs and utilize email, instant messaging, or video conferencing as needed.

 **Aimee**

One of my most successful strategies has been holding virtual open office hours. This practice began during the pandemic and has allowed me to support a diverse group of educators worldwide. I continue to offer these sessions to my new coaching team and plan to do so this year.

Open office hours provide a convenient and accessible way for individuals to get assistance. Schedule a consistent time on a digital video platform like Zoom, Google Meet, or Microsoft Teams; participants can then drop in virtually for support.

The experiences I've had with open office hours have been truly inspiring. When I started offering them, I wasn't sure what to expect. However, I've witnessed participants seeking help and supporting one another over time. It's been amazing to see this collaborative community develop.

Chapter 11

When Foundational Cracks Occur in Coaching
~ Assessing the Structure ~

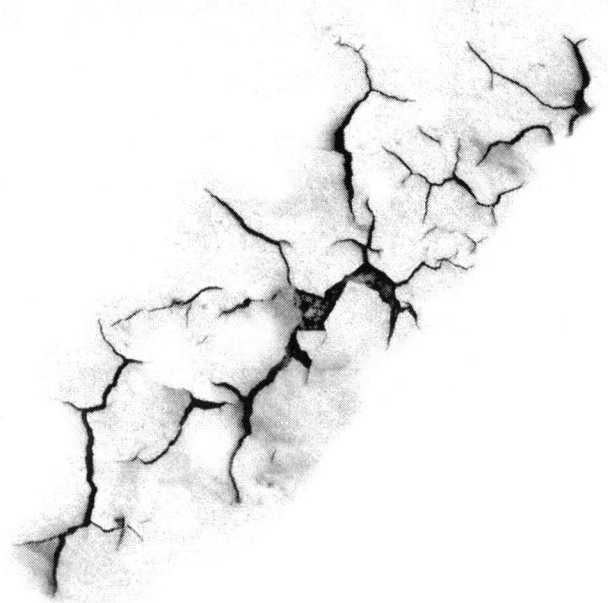

"Modern architecture does not mean the use of immature new materials; the main thing is to refine materials in a more human direction."

—**Alvar Aalto** (architect)

As an educational technology coach, you serve as a guide, much like a sherpa, helping to seamlessly integrate technology into education, akin to conquering Mount Everest. You aim to offer guidance and additional support as needed while allowing for independent successes, triumphs, and challenges. As we have previously discussed, coaching is where your creativity and critical thinking will thrive, and it is where you will experience significant professional growth as you navigate the unique challenges of being in a role that is typically a "teacher on special assignment," or as Aimee likes to say, "Fadmin" (Fake-admin).

This is an opportune moment to begin tracking your progress and reflecting on what has been effective for you in terms of engagement and your ability to coach through a feedback loop. Sometimes, though, our best intentions suddenly come to a halt when we face inevitable obstacles in our field.

As an educational technology coach, there are exhilarating moments and some challenging situations that might make you question your profession. Have you heard the saying "teachers are worse than students" regarding coaching, training, and demanding undivided attention? Is it intriguing to initiate a workshop where you ask educators to leave their cell phones in a box at the front of the room?

Just kidding!

Or are we?

This chapter is dedicated to helping you navigate through inevitable tough times. While we can't predict every challenge you may face in your educational environment, we can identify the top inevitable situations and provide support and suggestions.

Like David Letterman used to do, let's discuss the ten most inevitable situations or roadblocks you may encounter, along with possible solutions for each. In no particular order of importance ...

Number 10: Limited technology resources

Don't blame the teacher if your tech is slow, glitchy, or can't even load a cat video; blame the terrible equipment.

Tip

Advocate for increased technology budgets, explore grant opportunities and build partnerships with community organizations to supplement resources. Prioritize essential tools and provide training on maximizing their use.

Additional Tip!

Establish a technology lending library or sharing program among teachers to optimize resource utilization.

Laurie

I was hosting a training once with a group of social studies teachers. We looked at ways to engage and motivate students to do the work. The internet went down in the middle of the training. Like, totally down. Full stop, do not pass go, you are DONE. At that point, a seventh-grade teacher panicked. Having been in this situation before, I pivoted to a hands-on approach from my "bag of tricks" and continued with the presentation. Little time was wasted for me to pivot. That teacher, however, lost his ... well, you know what I mean. He said that this was the reason he didn't use technology. He went on to say it's unreliable and that he doesn't have the wherewithal to pivot.

So, even though I pivoted and could have gone on as planned, I needed to fully stop, and address the elephant in the room. Things happen. Technology fails. Or worse yet, we build something on one tech tool only to have the district not support it the year after. Sometimes, even when a goal is in sight, things go wrong. You need to be prepared for these moments and look for ways to overcome them —or better yet, find ways to work in harmony with this ever-changing landscape.

 Number 9: Lack of time

Teachers are expected to be tech wizards and busy putting out fires in the classroom. It's like asking a firefighter to moonwalk between blazes.

 **Tip**

Prioritizing tasks, delegating responsibilities, and using time management techniques are important. Focus on high-impact activities and help teachers become more self-sufficient. Set clear, achievable goals for both short-term and long-term planning. To ensure effective communication, maintain open and honest communication about time constraints and priorities.

Be prepared to adapt to unexpected challenges and schedule changes, and create a flexible coaching schedule that accommodates teachers' needs and availability.

Laurie

The number one complaint I hear when suggesting a way to use technology in the classroom is the need for more time to train and teach on the tool. As a tech integrator, coach, mentor, or whatever your title is, sometimes finding ways to save teachers time is the most effective way you can help. Teachers lack time. It's a fact. They have so much to get done every single day. A fifth-grade teacher once asked me to come into her classroom to teach a new tool. The idea was that she wanted her students to each create a slide that showcased their research. They were still writing the paper, but she thought having the students create visuals would help deepen the learning. Well, she wasn't wrong! She told me I had 15 minutes to teach students how to use the tool so that she could get them to work.

I arrived at the class and got all the students signed in to the tool. From there, I told them, "Go ahead and see if you can create one slide all about yourself. Be sure to add text, one still image, an animated image, and a short video where you describe something about yourself." I set a timer for 5 minutes and set them free. The teacher balked immediately. How would they do this without me walking them through each step? They need more guidance, she exclaimed.

So I told her to give them the 5 minutes. She and I walked around encouraging students to push all the buttons and to rely on each other when they figured something out. By the end of the 5 minutes, students had all created a basic all-about-me slide. They taught each other features and even found a few things that taught me a thing or two! After that, we got to work on creating the slides that were the teacher's learning objective. Instead of carving out 15 minutes from her lesson, I saved her 10. It's a small amount of time, but these minutes matter.

Not only did I save her time, but I also showcased the release of control when learning. She could shave time off many of her lessons just by allowing her students 5 minutes of exploration. This also fosters students' critical thinking, problem-solving, and communication skills, which is a win!

mber 8: Lack of administrative support

Tech initiatives without strong leadership support are like ships without captains: doomed to drift aimlessly and eventually sink.

Tip

Communicate the benefits of technology integration to administrators, using data to show its impact on student achievement. Establish strong relationships with school leaders and involve them in technology initiatives.

Additional Tip

Develop a shared vision for technology integration that aligns with school goals in collaboration with your administration.

Laurie

Do you know the mission and vision of your school district? If not, put this book down and pull up your school's website. Give it a read. If it is important enough to put on the site, then it is important enough to your administration. You can almost guarantee support if you align what you are trying to achieve with that mission and vision statement. The problem is often when these two things don't align or the administration isn't willing to walk the walk. Both Aimee and I are in administrative roles now, so we can see where communication can break down between both sides.

I worked for a fantastic administrator when I first took on the coaching role. He stepped back and supported my crazy ideas but would push my thinking and question things when they didn't align with his vision for my role. For example, when I was first a coach, I thought my room could be used for teacher training and as a makerspace. I had all new furniture, flexible seating, two new interactive boards, large whiteboards, and tons of storage. I was ready to buy a ton of manipulatives, consumables, robotics, books—you name it! I came armed with ideas on how to make it work.

I got a resounding no, not just from him but from the business official who approved the purchase of the new furniture: Students were by no means allowed into the space; it was for teachers only. I was flabbergasted and frustrated. But, through discussions, we agreed. I kept the room kid-free for the first year and supported the librarians in putting a makerspace in their libraries. All of it was scaled back from my grand ideas, but it helped me see the priorities and vision the administration had for my role.

In year two, I brought students into the space in a limited fashion, where they could use the ample floor space for robotics that would not work in their classrooms. Since PD was the priority, I showed teachers how to bring robotics and creativity into their classrooms with my support.

Number 7: Privacy laws

Keeping tabs on student data is like herding cats in a digital jungle. It's a full-time job, especially when trying to be a tech-savvy trailblazer.

Tip

In this digital age, we must protect our information and privacy and the students we serve. To ensure compliance, check with your technology director, local agencies, and platform privacy statements. Moreover, adhere to your school's vetted list of acceptable apps and platforms.

 **Aimee**

As someone who likes to shake up the "status quo," I understand the frustration of sticking to a limited list of safe, educational apps while trying to bring innovation to education. There are many free and enjoyable applications available, but we need to consider the potential risks. When students mindlessly accept an application's terms of service without reading them, they are inadvertently granting access to their personal information. This information is precious, and we should do all we can within our educational institutions to protect students' identities.

As mentioned in this book, Laurie and I are both currently located in New York State, where we have a student privacy law called EdLaw 2-d that safeguards student data and privacy. This law requires a contract between educational vendors and schools outlining how the vendor collects and uses student data. Educators and administrators must exclusively utilize software applications approved and agreed upon by the school and the vendor.

As a former instructional technology coordinator for BOCES, I've seen firsthand the challenges educators face in protecting student data privacy. One recurring theme I encountered was a lack of understanding about how cloud-based applications work, particularly single sign-on (SSO) solutions.

During a meeting with tech guru representatives from various schools I oversaw regarding instructional technology, a discussion about data privacy and security arose. It became clear that there were misconceptions about how SSO systems function. For instance, one teacher, "a tech guru representative," believed that using SSO to access an application meant the school had a contract with that specific vendor, ensuring data protection.

Unfortunately, this was a common misconception. I explained that SSO provides convenience but doesn't automatically guarantee data privacy. When a school uses SSO to access an application, it is essentially granting that application permission to access student data. This is why verifying with your educational institution which apps and websites are approved for use is important. Some educational tools may not adhere to the necessary protocols for protecting student data, which could expose sensitive information. Therefore, checking for approved resources can help ensure student data remains secure.

To illustrate the importance of data privacy, I used the analogy of parental responsibility. When we allow our children to use apps or websites, we act as their digital guardians, responsible for safeguarding their information.

The risks of data breaches are real. Students can become victims of identity theft, with credit cards and loans opened in their names before they even reach their teens. It's a frightening reality but one that educators must confront.

As responsible parties in the educational system, it is our duty to protect student data privacy. This includes carefully evaluating the privacy policies of cloud-based applications, ensuring contracts are established if required by your state, understanding how SSO (single sign-on) works, and educating teachers and staff about the potential risks. By taking these steps, we can help ensure that our students' personal information remains safe in the digital age.

Number 6: Teachers at different levels

Tech-savvy teachers are like a beacon of hope in a sea of digital confusion. They're the ones who can navigate the stormy waters.

This is an excellent time to survey your teachers as soon as possible to understand their current situation and how you can meet their needs. After developing a survey and collecting responses, you can devise a plan for appropriate workshops and coaching cycles.

Laurie

Just as students are different in your classrooms, your PD sessions will have teachers at all levels, too! I use the rule of three for any hands-on activities when training a larger group. Any time I want teachers to try something out, I offer three options. I am using UDL strategies by offering choice, but I am also trying to give teachers an entry point based on their comfort zones and preferences. Whenever teachers are learning something new during my training, I also use something that I call the 411 method. Why do I call it that? We call 411 for information, and the same context fits here. This method gives me a chance to survey the room based on how things went and gives teachers a safe place to try things out. The 411 method allows learning through exploration, reflection, and inquiry and breaks down the learning process into manageable segments.

4-1-1 Exploration
Template

Here's how it works: The first 4 minutes are spent exploring whatever you want the teachers to learn. This is done after logins but before you dive into the features. Then, teachers have 1 minute to jot down what they learned, and in the last minute, they jot down questions they have. From there, you debrief.

By using this method, you can guarantee that you meet the needs of all learners because you have a better understanding of their starting point.

Number 5: Standardization—Including scripted curriculum and inclusion

Trying to fit technology into a rigid curriculum is like squeezing a square peg into a round hole—it takes a lot of creativity and duct tape.

**Tip**

Encourage teachers to integrate technology into their lessons to enhance learning outcomes rather than trying to fit technology into existing curriculum structures. This can be done by incorporating personalized learning, digitizing collaboration, and using technology for digital assessments and feedback. Take the time to sit and converse with curriculum leaders at grade-level meetings.

Teachers lead to understanding the curriculum assessment gaps and have a foundation for what is expected from the curriculum. This is the time to really lean into UDL and the technology frameworks discussed earlier in the book.

Plus, if you can showcase how teachers can make the learning stick because you integrate the technology AND that it won't take extra time, you will get past the teachers feeling like their hands are tied to their pacing guides.

Laurie

This is definitely one of my biggest hurdles. I work with over 30 districts, each using different curriculums with varying amounts of fidelity. Even as a seasoned coach, I still struggle with this, as it is ever-present, and the target keeps shifting. But I've had a few wins that I'd consider small but mighty. The best advice I can give you here is that you may need to prove the "why" before determining the "how."

Why does technology integration help? Well, engagement, critical thinking, creativity, and communication—you name it—will be increased if you use interactive tools and multimedia resources. Technology can personalize learning for students. And if you can make it real-world relevant, you can increase learning exponentially for students. The "why" for teachers is in the efficiency, data, and flexibility technology can offer within their teaching constraints.

The "how"? Well, find ways in! One district I am lucky enough to work with has a STEAM bus. This was built in 2020 to get students out of the classrooms and to connect with the community. When I'm on the bus, I set up stations for the students to rotate through. I ask their teachers to float and support students in their exploration. It is a time for them to learn the technology, see the engagement, and ask questions. For me, it's like a half-hour advertisement for all the good technology can do. From there, I try to showcase how these tech tools can support classroom learning. If I get asked to come into the classroom to extend the learning, I count it as a win!

Number 4: Workload and teachers' well-being

Balancing the demands of teaching with the need for self-care is like trying to ride a unicycle on a tightrope. It's time to get off the tightrope and find a safer way to get around.

 **Tip**

Remember to be an active listener above all else. When working with educators, listen to their concerns, worries, and what they consider to be their strengths and weaknesses. Actively respond with intention. Offer support systems and ensure that working norms are addressed. Be empathetic. Encourage time-management strategies and meet the teachers at a level they are comfortable with when using technology. Remember to celebrate successes and wins and to provide ongoing support.

 **Aimee**

Teacher burnout is a very real issue. Like our students, we bring our own stress and anxiety into the classroom, whether we realize it our not, often neglecting to take care of ourselves in this constantly connected world.

At one point in my career, I had multiple roles at a private school with approximately 450 students. I loved being a part of the entire school community as I was the "Student and Technology Services Coordinator," a union-friendly term for someone who did not yet possess an admin degree for an assistant principal or director of technology, and teaching computer classes to two sections of preschool through eighth-grade students.

On top of that, I was also a mom and my children attended the same school. My days were filled with student issues, ensuring server security, teaching classes, coaching teachers, and juggling family responsibilities. I was always on call, even during vacations, as I was solely responsible for our network's safety and security. It all became too much, especially when my mother fell ill, and I found myself struggling to balance caring for her, my family, and work.

I remember one night feeling overwhelmed, as I couldn't keep up with the balance. My chest was pounding, I was unable to catch my breath, and I thought I was having a heart attack. During that period, I lost a lot of weight. I felt like I was drowning and couldn't do anything well.

It was a dark time for me. Balancing life and work was difficult, and worst of all, I was losing myself. What did I do? Well, the journey to feeling like me was long and life-changing. I began small. I stopped checking my email after 5 p.m. and started taking brisk, short walks during work. I prioritized my time, and most importantly, I prioritized myself. I started running again and eventually sought to talk to someone professionally.

Now that this is in text, it seems like such an easy transition, like I just woke up one day and said this is what I need to do to be healthy. Please know that it wasn't. It took years for me to finally realize that at the end of the day if I am not healthy enough to take care of myself, how am I going to take care of anyone else? I spoke before about moments; please take those moments to take care of you.

Number 3: Digital citizenship gaps

Teachers, let's ditch the "fear" and embrace the "fun" of technology! You're the digital superheroes your students need. Teach them how to be responsible, ethical, and totally awesome online. Let's revolutionize the future together!

Tip

Often, teachers or administrators hesitate to allow their students to use technology because they fear it will not be used for the greater good. Digital citizenship is a skill that needs to be nurtured and demonstrated, and it's the perfect opportunity for you to provide comprehensive training for the educators and administration with whom you work.

Yes, you can play a vital role in implementing digital citizenship lessons. However, digital citizenship is not a one-and-done lesson. Instead, it should be integrated into every classroom regardless of age or subject matter being taught. You must incorporate digital citizenship practices encompassing online communication, data and privacy protection, and proper use of online resources. Good digital citizenship starts with you and how you model its practices.

**Laurie**

There are many debates about locking and blocking, what students should have access to, and which tech tools are OK for students to use. I like to tell the story of one of my early years in the classroom to showcase what happens in these situations. It was when Instagram had just come on the scene. My classroom was 1:1 with iPads, and we used them often in class, utilizing apps like Nearpod to get students to interact with technology.

A girl in my sixth-grade class came to me in tears one morning. She said that another student told her there were pictures of her on Instagram of her in the locker room changing. Because she was only 11, she told me that social media was not allowed for her and that her parents had strict rules that prohibited social media before age 13. She felt she had no recourse to take down the photos or even see them. The administration took over the investigation and determined what should have happened to the culprits who had used their phones to take pictures of her without her knowing.

For me, though, it was a wake-up call. I had to teach my students about using the technology I freely used in the classroom. We needed guardrails far beyond what was being blocked. We needed to help students harness the technology they had in their pockets. Parents were new to this, too, so they had no idea how to help their children. I started using the Common Sense Education Digital Citizenship lessons built into Nearpod that year (scan QR code for more information). I learned alongside my students about the dangers and discoveries that technology offers. We had open conversations about ethics, bias, safety, and our footprints.

Digital Citizenship
Schuylerville CSD

When I moved to my first coaching role, I taught digital citizenship K–12. I hosted parent nights and spent time building strong digital citizenship skills with students beyond being about what to block or whether cell phones should be allowed in schools. Digital citizenship is about how to be a good human in a digital world. Taking away devices will help with attention and focus in your classrooms, but it doesn't prepare students to use the technology safely when they have access. Open access allows students to make mistakes that go far beyond the walls of their schools, making it vital that you teach students about ethical behavior.

You have to teach students how to be creators instead of just consumers. You have to prepare students to think critically about what they see online and to think before they post. And you have to help your students know what to do when something happens. This is especially true around cyberbullying. While coaching, you should model good citizenship and help build the capacity for teaching these essential topics in all classrooms daily.

Number 2: Codependency

Sometimes, a teacher might become too dependent on their tech coach. It's like being the teacher's tech superhero! But remember, it's a sign of their trust and appreciation. And who doesn't love being a superhero?

Tip

You may have the best intentions, but sometimes, things can fall short for various reasons. At some point in your career, you may encounter an educator who doesn't fulfill their part of the coaching partnership. This could be due to a lack of communication or a fear of working alone. Always assume the best intentions, even if the educator takes advantage of your expertise for extra planning time.

So, what can you do? Sometimes, it's helpful to go back to basics and recalibrate. Your best defense can be being open and honest about your concerns and transparent about how you view the partnership. Revisit the norms you established and be an active listener if any issues arise.

On the other hand, you may have a teacher with whom you work well. Before you know it, you may spend much time working with that person. This isn't necessarily a bad thing, but it's important to share the workload. One way to handle this is to have that teacher serve as an example, assisting you in presenting and sharing their knowledge and expertise. By taking them under your wing, you can allow them to shine, which can help you attract more clients.

 **Aimee**

Years back, when I was newer to the coaching role, I had an eye-opening experience supporting a colleague with project-based learning and integrating technology. At first, I was doing everything right by providing guidance and feedback. I followed the coaching cycle, set up collaborative norms, and completed feedback loops. However, I realized that my colleague was becoming overly reliant on me, to the point of leaving the classroom for breaks while I took over. It was a wake-up call to adjust my approach and empower my colleague to take the lead.

My colleague shared her anxieties in a candid meeting about entering a more prominent role. We realized that our initial plan was not effectively addressing her concerns. So, we took a step back, revisited our goals, and reworked our plan to ensure she felt confident and empowered to lead the learning process. It was a crucial turning point in our collaboration and a learning experience for both of us.

And the most unavoidable roadblock is, even though this is in no particular order...

Number 1: Resistance to change/keeping up with emerging tech/fear of trying something new

Change is like learning a new dance move. It may be awkward initially, but you'll be a pro in no time with practice.

**Tip**

Embracing change can be challenging, even for the most adaptable. A growth mindset is crucial. Consider hosting a seminar or workshop to cultivate this mindset. Stay ahead of the curve by sharing newsletters on emerging technologies like AI and how they can revolutionize your workplace.

Provide educators with opportunities to experiment with new tools and determine their best fit for the classroom. Celebrate successes when a teacher takes the bold step to embrace new technology. Foster a collaborative culture where educators can share ideas, learn from each other, and work together to solve problems. Most importantly, meet teachers where they are and develop their skills at a pace with which they are most comfortable.

One effective method to encourage a hesitant teacher to try new things is to start with small, manageable steps. Rather than overwhelming them with an entirely new lesson plan, suggest integrating a single technology tool into an existing lesson. This will enable them to experiment with technology in a less intimidating way and gradually build their confidence. Ensure you are available for ongoing support, be an active listener, and provide tutorials with visuals to help support when you cannot be present.

Aimee

In 2006, during my second year of teaching art and computer classes at a private school for preschool through eighth grade, I was asked to serve as an unofficial "educational technology coach." At the time, we only had one computer classroom, and I was tasked with teaching the teachers how to use Microsoft Excel as a grade book. This was challenging because, in 2006, we were still using paper for report cards and grade books.

I decided that the best way for the teachers to understand how to use the Microsoft Excel spreadsheet I created was for them to participate and play along. So, during the workshop introduction, I greeted the teachers, which I took for granted that I already knew, and projected the grade book I created for the school on the wall using a projector from a wobbly table and began explaining its functions. As I went through the demonstration, one of the teachers expressed his frustration and disbelief about using computers in his classroom, let alone for a gradebook. He feverishly got up and walked out of the room—out of the building and across the street—to smoke a cigarette.

The entire room fell silent as I attempted to dust myself off and pick up from where I left off, trying to pay no attention to the man smoking a cigarette and watching from across the street.

Wait! What did I do wrong? I questioned myself as I continued. I mean, I knew he wasn't exactly tech-savvy, as I remember countless times teaching him how to log into his email. However, I greatly misunderstood just how resistant he was.

This experience made me realize that I had failed to understand the teachers' perspective and their level of expertise. I assumed I knew everyone in the room because they were my colleagues. I also thought I'd covered all of my bases because I hand-delivered their "why." From then on, I prioritized understanding the learners in the room before giving professional development sessions to teachers. I started taking surveys and grouping the teachers based on their comfort levels. This approach has been more effective in getting teachers to engage in professional development sessions.

Since that incident, I can proudly say that I have not had a teacher walk out of my professional development sessions (sessions at conferences are a different beast, and you learn not to take it personally since attendees often hop from one session to another). I have also learned to read the room and adapt my approach to engage the participants better. I have learned that it is OK to do checkpoints halfway through and return to the basics by allowing time for play and self-exploration.

To this day, I can still see this man standing across the street, arms folded, puffing on a cigarette. I'd like to think that he was still interested because he appeared to be staring into the window from across the street, continuing to watch me and not attempting to taunt me.

After carefully reviewing the list and exploring our stories, take time to recognize the most challenging obstacles you have faced. Reflect on whether additional issues still need to be addressed in the list. This is a good time for self-reflection and thoughtful planning to overcome these obstacles and any others that may arise in your current situation. Challenges like the ones mentioned above are often unavoidable. Remember to stay positive and, when faced with a challenge, focus on your reasons for pursuing your goals, keep your plan in mind, and move forward with determination.

Conclusion

ArchiTeching the Future of EdTech Coaching

Creativity is "an idea that is novel, good, and useful. Making connections between different ideas to solve a new problem."

—**Michael Grybko** (neuroscientist)

So, after reading this far, you're super organized with your calendar and have set up a booking calendar. You have your coaching logs ready and your SMART goals aligned. You're officially ready to be of service to others! You know it is also important to prioritize YOUR professional development to stay updated on the latest educational technology trends and best practices. Hopefully, you plan to attend conferences, webinars, or workshops to expand your knowledge and skills. Make sure to mark important dates from ISTE, FETC, TCEA (Texas Computer Education Association), or any other educational technology organization's conferences and professional development dates in your calendar.

Remember, it is crucial to prioritize self-care. It is important to make time for regular breaks, manage stress effectively, and prioritize your well-being to maintain optimum productivity.

Building Futures: A Reflection on the Journey or "The Blueprint Complete: A Look Forward"

OK, now what? You took the journey with us, and for that, we thank you! But we also know that the journey isn't over; the important chapter is about to begin. You need to do the work, implement what you learned, and try things beyond your comfort zone. There will probably be several moments where you go, hmm, what would Aimee and Laurie do in this situation? And for that, we say it's all about you now. You have the tools, you have the stories, and you have the know-how. How you go forward now is up to you.

But remember, you are not alone in this journey. You took the first few miles with us, but there are miles to go, my friend, and we are right there with you. We do this work with love, and we do it daily. It takes up our weeks and often our weekends.

We have met together so many times late in the evening, laughing at our errors, bouncing ideas off each other, and sharing stories. While it was exhausting and took way longer than initially planned, we are both better for it.

Coaching is a team sport, and we are your cheerleaders. This is just the beginning, and you get to write the rest! But we didn't write all this without giving you a call to action.

We need to pause and reflect on the themes discussed in this book. At the beginning, we said this is not a manual on educational technology but rather a blueprint for empowering you and those you support, fostering creativity, and driving meaningful change in your schools. It's all about making sure we are equipped to support our students and offer the best learning opportunities. At the heart of every interaction you will have while coaching lies a profound opportunity to help educators and students grow, connect, and see the possibilities.

The Role of the EdTech Coach

Throughout the beginning chapters, we explored an EdTech coach's many roles: facilitator, connector, collaborator, leader, and innovator. As an architect of change, you will design learning experiences, shape professional learning experiences, and create creative learning environments that help others thrive. Your role goes beyond the tool or even a strategy. It is up to you to build a culture of curiosity, resilience, and innovation for your districts and your classrooms.

Creativity in an EdTech Role

Creativity is a theme you see woven through this entire book. We explored our feelings about it and shared our creative experiences. For you, it is about finding new ways to engage your teachers and exploring the endless possibilities that educational technology can support. Creativity is the core of all that we do. We ask you to consider your relationship with creativity and consider how to bring creativity into your coaching practice.

Continuous Improvement

While creativity is the core, the commitment to continuous improvement is your call to action—both for the educators you support and yourself. Use feedback loops, look at the data, measure engagement, evaluate your progress, and empower others to learn from you. Don't be static. You are not a statue, but rather the clay constantly being molded and hopefully not smashed! This work is ever-evolving, and you will always be adapting. Just strive to meet these ever-changing needs of students and educators alike.

Collaboration and Community

We keep saying it, but it is true: You are only as strong as those around you. Establish your PLN either by joining one or creating one. Collaboration is key to success; you can't coach in a silo. Get out there and build those relationships and work together to foster growth. Learn to rely on your network for support, advice, and, most of all, as a catalyst for your own growth and success.

Looking Ahead

The challenges and opportunities of being an educational technology coach have never been greater, and they will continue to evolve. Embrace the ups and downs that this role can offer. Everything is a fleeting moment, and in that moment, there is so much to learn from. Your work is critical in shaping how educators use technology in their classrooms. You will remain at the forefront of educational innovation by staying creative, adaptive, and collaborative.

Final Words

Let's be real. We embrace fun as often as we can. We find ways to smile, laugh, and be silly as often as we can. Find us at a conference, and we are probably wearing crazy shirts or costumes with our friend Deann. Our PLN will always be larger than the two of us, and we look forward to the times when our EDU pals can be together.

So while the work is tough, and we encourage you to roll up your sleeves and get stuff done, remember to embrace the journey. As you continue to architech learning experiences, empower educators, and drive change, remember that you are not just building lesson plans or throwing tech tools into classrooms; you are shaping young minds and exciting teachers one innovative way at a time.

So embrace that creative genius we know is inside you. Listen to those you coach (even when they don't know they need it), and push boundaries. The blueprint may be complete, but the real work? It is just getting started. Go change the world ... we will be right here watching!

The next chapter is up to you ...

Resources

Are you overwhelmed with all the awesomeness? ~ Unlock the chapter resources for your book by scanning the QR code below! ~

"We are drowning in information but starved for knowledge."

— **John Naisbitt** (author, speaker)

Identity Automation is a leading provider of identity management and security solutions tailored for education. Streamlining access and enhancing security, we empower EdTech Coaches to concentrate on enriching the learning experience rather than restrictions due to data safety. With features like user-friendly Single Sign-On (SSO) and delegated password resets, coaches can facilitate seamless collaboration among educators and students, creating a space that encourages new ideas and creativity. Our robust anti-phishing protection and network monitoring further ensure that digital interactions remain secure, allowing educators to focus on mentoring and transforming educational practices. Ultimately, Identity Automation equips EdTech Coaches with the tools they need to create a safe and productive digital classroom, promoting both trust and success in the learning process.

**Compromised
Credential Check**

**Student-Teacher
Portal**

**Benefits
of PhishID**

Identity
Automation

www.identityautomation.com

Our vision is to empower educators by amplifying their voices and fostering a culture where their expertise, insights, and experiences are valued and utilized to drive positive change in education. We envision a collaborative community where educators are recognized as key stakeholders and actively engaged in shaping our publications, podcasts, professional development, and partnerships.

Through platforms for advocacy, professional development, and networking, we aim to cultivate a supportive environment where educators feel empowered to share their knowledge, innovate, and advocate for equitable, inclusive, and impactful educational experiences for all learners. Together, we strive to elevate educators' voices to inspire a brighter future for education.

Our mission is to foster a culture of unity and collaboration where every individual's unique strengths and perspectives are celebrated and leveraged for collective growth.

Through inclusivity, empathy, and respect, we strive to create an environment where diversity is embraced as a source of strength. We are committed to cultivating meaningful connections, empowering each other to reach our full potential, and creating positive change in our communities. Together, we believe in the power of solidarity to overcome challenges, inspire innovation, and build a brighter, more equitable future for all.

View our services, catalog of books, and meet our community of educators at
https://xfactoredu.org

Kid Series

Leadership Series

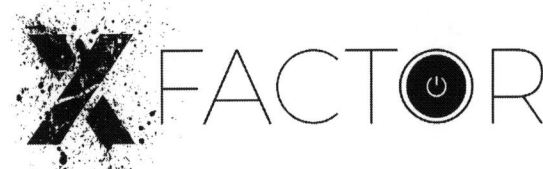

Made in the USA
Middletown, DE
29 November 2025